DEMENTIA PRAECOX

DR.   C.G. JUNG

PRIVATE DOCENT IN PSYCHIATRY, UNIVERSITY OF ZURICH

AUTHORIZED TRANSLATION WITH AN INTRODUCTION

BY

FREDERICK PETERSON, M.D.

PROFESSOR OF PSYCHIATRY, COLUMBIA UNIVERSITY, NEW YORK

AND

A. A. BRILL, PH.B., M.D.

ASSISTANT IN PSYCHIATRY, COLUMBIA UNIVERSITY, NEW YORK

ISBN: 978-1-63923-803-3

Printed: March 2023

Published and Distributed By:
Lushena Books
607 Country Club Drive, Unit E
Bensenville, IL 60106
www.lushenabks.com

ISBN: 978-1-63923-803-3

CONTENTS.

TRANSLATORS' INTRODUCTION.

To Kraepelin belongs the credit of having introduced new life into psychiatry by his indefatigable study of his patients for long years, his keen clinical insight, and especially by an independence of thought which led him to fearlessly shatter the traditions of centuries as regards the classification of mental diseases. As a pupil of Wundt he was able to apply new methods of clinical investigation drawn from psychology. As is well known he has brought together mania and melancholia as a single disorder under the title manic-depressive insanity. This conception, vigorously attacked at first, has probably come to stay. It is otherwise with his creation of dementia præcox, which is still strongly objected to in many quarters, chiefly because it seems to be a kind of waste basket into which are thrown all forms of mental disease that cannot be tagged with another name. This disorder appears in so many guises that it is already divided into hebephrenic, catatonic and paranoid groups, and Kraepelin himself has intimated that in time it will be broken up into still further groups or types. It is his merit, however, to have placed before us this psychological species even if the outlines are gross and the details more or less obscure.

In following Kraepelin we find that he only offers us a general and superficial view of the disease. From his description we learn that the patients are peculiar in speech and actions, that they utter numerous senseless remarks, repeat meaningless words or syllables, and that now and then they commit foolish and impulsive acts, but no attempt is made to examine the nature and origin of these peculiar utterances and actions. When we review the cases described in Kraepelin's works we find that whereas most of them show hallucinations and delusions, these are not at all of the same content or nature; the verbigerations and mannerisms, too, differ in different cases. The same similarities and divergences are to be noticed in every hospital. We recall a patient whose auditory hallucinations were attributed to a child, and another who heard the voice of God. The mannerisms of one were characterized by a continuous rubbing on the top of his head, while another for hours described certain figures in the air. Are these diversities accidental or have they a reason? Is there any difference between Kraepelin's patient who saw a blue heart up above, and behind it quivering sunshine and another blue heart, " a little woman's heart,"[1] and the patient who[2] lived by the word of God, a raven was at the window who wished to eat his flesh; or between the patient who repeated numerous times the same unintelligible sentences " one for all and all for one, and two for all and three for all," etc.,[3] and the patient who speaks about " a poinard with a nuptial note "?[4] The same questions could be asked about the manifold so-called senseless actions of patients. Kraepelin makes no attempt to explain these senseless utterances and actions. In other words, whereas he gives us an accurate, almost photographic account of the patient's general behavior, he does not enter into his psychological productions. He contents himself with noting that the patient entertains such and such hallucinations and delusions, and such and such mannerisms, without examining the causal relations. Those who work among the insane know that no two cases of dementia præcox are alike; there is always a difference in the grouping and relationship of the symptoms, every case having its own individuality. Kraepelin, like his predecessors, totally ignores individual psychology, a thing absolutely essential for the understanding of the psychosis, just as the microscope is for pathology. The present difficulties in classification are mainly due to a lack of knowledge of the influence of individuality without which no real classification is possible.

Bleuler[5] and Jung[6] inaugurated a new epoch in psychiatry by attempting to penetrate into the mysteries of the individual influence of the symptoms. They show conclusively why we have here this combination and there that combination of symptoms. In the cases described by them we see that the senseless expres-

[1] Kraepelin: Psychiatrische Klinik, p. 29.
[2] Ibid., p. 26.
[3] Ibid., p. 37.
[4] Kraepelin: Psychiatrie, Vol. II, p. 152.
[5] Bleuler: Affektivität, Suggestibilität, Paranoia, Marhold, Halle.
[6] Jung: Über die Psychologie der Dementia Præcox, Marhold, Halle.

sions and actions have their reasons. But both Bleuler and Jung[7] are only pioneers in a new field; they are not the discoverers of this *terra incognita*. The honor of this belongs to Breuer and Freud.

In 1895 Breuer and Freud published the "Studien über Hysterie,"[8] in which they showed that hysterical symptoms were symbolic representations of individual experiences which were incompatible with the personality and hence repressed from consciousness. This will be best illustrated by an abstract of a case described by Freud in the aforesaid work.[9]

Miss Lucy R., thirty years old, had been treated by a specialist for purulent rhinitis. Some time after she again applied for treatment; this time, however, she suffered from complete anosmia and was almost constantly annoyed by two subjective sensations of smell. She was also depressed and anergic, complained of a heavy head, loss of appetite and inability to work. As no local affection could then be found to account for these symptoms she was recommended to Freud.

Besides the symptoms enumerated above Freud found distinct hysterical symptoms. She showed a general analgesia without any disturbances of tactile sensation. The nasal mucous membrane was totally analgesic and its reflexes absent. Freud then thought that the subjective sensations of smell and the depression were equivalents for hysterical attacks, that those odors were once objective and due to some trauma, and that they returned to memory in the form of symbols of subjective sensation. But in order to assume this theory it was absolutely necessary that the subjective sensations of smell should show such a specialization as to correspond with the real object of their origin. When the patient was asked to describe the odor which annoyed her most, she stated that it was like "burned pastry." It was therefore assumed that the odor of burned pastry was probably some actual traumatic experience. Her history was uneventful; she was a governess, having the care of two children whose mother died a few years ago, the father being a manufacturer in the suburbs of Vienna. The odor of burned pastry was taken as the

[7] Jung: Diagnostische Associationsstudien, Barth, Leipzig.
[8] Breuer and Freud: Studien über Hysterie, Deuticke, Leipzig und Wien.
[9] *Ibid.*, p. 90.

starting point for the analysis. Employing the method of continuous associations the patient was asked to concentrate her
mind on the odor of burned pastry and then tell under what circumstances it originated. After long and persevering labor she
finally recalled that it occurred about two months before. It was
just two days before her birthday. She was with the two children (girls) in the school room teaching them to cook when a
letter was brought to her from her mother in Glasgow. The
children grasped the letter, remarking that it was probably a
birthday congratulation and they would keep it until her birthday.
While the children were thus bickering they forgot the pastry
which they were cooking and it was burned. Since that time
she had perceived that odor almost constantly and it was generally enhanced on excitement. When asked why she was then
excited she answered that " the children were so attached to her."
They were always attached to her, but just then she received a
letter from her mother. When asked to explain the contrast
produced by the attachment of the children and her mother's
letter, she stated that at that time she had intended to go home
to her mother and had a heavy heart at the thought of leaving
the children. To the question why she wished to leave her position, she stated that things were unbearable. She no longer lived
in harmony with the other servants because they imagined that
she considered herself too proud for her position. They said
many things to her employers about her and when she complained she was not upheld. She then decided to resign and
spoke about it to her employer. He was quite friendly and
advised her to reconsider it. It was while she was in that state
of indecision that the incident with the letter took place. Besides
that she was a distant relative to the mother of the children who
on her death bed asked her to care for the children and " take
the place of their mother." When she was to resign she entertained many scruples about breaking this promise.

This apparently analyzes the subjective sensation of smell. It
was really once an objective sensation and intimately associated
with an experience in which there was a play of contrary affects,
the sorrow at leaving the children and the mortification urging
her to that decision. The letter naturally recalled the motive of
this decision, because she thought of returning to her mother.

The conflict of affects raised this moment to a trauma and the sensation of smell which was connected with it remained as a symbol of it. The sense of smell is rarely made use of as a symbol, but in this case we know that she suffered from a chronic nasal affection and just then she suffered from severe coryza and could hardly smell anything; in her excitement, however, she perceived the odor of burned pastry.

As plausible as this sounded there was still something lacking. Freud asked himself why this conflict of affects should have led to hysteria, why did it not remain on a normal psychological basis; in other words, what justified this conversion? Previous experience showed that in all newly acquired hysterias one psychological determination is invariable, namely, that some presentation must intentionally be repressed from consciousness and excluded from psychical collaboration.

" In this intentional repression I also noticed the reason for the conversion of the sum of excitement, be it partial or total. The sum of excitation which cannot enter the psychic association thus finds the way to bodily innervation. The reason for the repression can only be a painful feeling. The repressed idea was incompatible with the ego. The repressed presentation avenges itself by becoming pathogenic."

From this he concluded that in the moment of hysterical conversion there must have been one trauma which she intentionally left in darkness. There was only one interpretation. He then told her that he believed that besides her attachment for the children she also loved her employer. Hesitatingly she answered, " Yes, I believe it is true." Asked why she did not mention this before she said, " Why, I didn't know it, or rather I did not wish to know it; I wanted to crowd it out of my head, never to think of it, and of late I was successful." After this admission all resistance was broken. She then related that during the first few years of her service she entertained no such wishes until one day when her master, a rather reserved and very busy man, talked confidentially with her concerning the rearing of the children. He was then more cordial than usual. He said that he counted on her to bring up his orphaned children and looked at her rather peculiarly. It was at this moment that she began to love him and entertain pleasant hopes. But, as this was not followed by anything else, and in spite of her long wait, he never gave her another confidential heart to heart talk, she tried " to push it out of her mind."

After this analysis there was some improvement, the subjective sensation became weaker, though it had not entirely disappeared, manifesting itself whenever she became excited. The persistence of this symbol was due to the fact that besides the main trauma it also represented many side traumas, so that it was necessary to analyze all episodes connected with the main scene. It finally disappeared, only to be replaced by another subjective odor " like the smoke of a cigar." As ungratifying as this was an immediate attempt was made to analyze it. When asked to recall the circumstances of the origin of this sensation she was at first unable to do so, remarking that the odor could be constantly perceived in the house, but finally under concentration she saw a picture of a table scene. It was in the dining room at dinner, where besides the usual company there was a guest, the chief accountant of the firm, an old gentleman who was a frequent visitor and who loved the children as though they were his grandchildren. While taking leave the visitor attempted to kiss the children when the host cried out, " Please don't kiss the children." " I then experienced a stitch in the heart, and as they were smoking this odor remained in my memory."

This therefore was the second scene causing the trauma and leaving the memory symbol. But why was this scene so affective? On analysis it was found that it preceded the burned pastry by about two months. It was not, however, obvious why she should have been so affected when the old gentleman was prevented from kissing the children. She stated that the father objected to strangers kissing the children, and that a few months before this episode a lady visited the house and on leaving kissed the children. At that time the father said nothing to the lady, but afterwards upbraided her for permitting it, saying that if it ever happened again he would entrust the bringing up of his children to some one else. This happened while she believed herself loved and soon expected a second confidential talk. This episode shattered all her hopes because if he could reproach her for a thing of which she was perfectly innocent he could not entertain any feeling for her. This painful incident was manifestly recalled when the bookkeeper attempted to kiss the children.

This ended the analysis and the patient was cured. A few days later the anosmia disappeared and the reflex returned.

This abstract shows very nicely how the symptoms were nothing other than painful psychical experiences symbolically converted into physical ones. The traumatic moment causing this conversion is that in which the contradiction thrusts itself on the ego and is therefore banished by it. The banishment does not annihilate the opposing presentation, but crowds it into the unconscious. This process occurring for the first time forms the nucleus and crystallization point for the formation of a psychic group separated from the ego, around which collects everything in accord with the contradictory presentation. The splitting of consciousness in such cases is intentional; it is often initiated by at least one arbitrary act. However something else happens than the individual intends; he wishes to eliminate a presentation as though it never came to pass, but only succeeds in isolating it psychically.

The traumatic moment in our patient corresponds to the time when she was upbraided by her master for allowing the children to be kissed. For the time being this episode remained without any apparent effects, perhaps it caused the depression and sensitiveness. The hysterical symptoms commenced later in moments which can be designated as "auxiliary" and which are characterized by a simultaneous flowing together of both psychical groups. The first moment in which the conversion took place in Miss Lucy was the scene at the table when the chief accountant attempted to kiss the children. This evoked the traumatic memory and she behaved as though she had not entirely banished her attachment for her master.

The second auxiliary moment almost followed the mechanism of the first. It is interesting to note how the symptom coming second covered the first so that it was not clearly distinguished until the former was eliminated, a thing quite usually observed in psychanalysis.

The therapy consisted in forcing the union of the split-off psychic groups with the ego-consciousness.

Similar conclusions were reached by Jung on the basis of experimental psychology.[10]

Jung and Riklin collected a great number of associations from normal persons with the intention of finding out first whether there exists any regularity in the reactions, and second whether there are definite reaction types. It was soon found that the process of association is an extraordinarily flighty and variable psychic process, and is under the influence of numberless psychical events which are beyond the limits of objective control. It was also found that attention exerts the greatest influence on the association process. It directs and modifies the associative process and at the same time can be most readily controlled by experiments. It is the delicate affective apparatus which is the first to react in abnormal physical and psychic conditions, thus modifying the associative accomplishments. It was therefore decided to investigate experimentally the following questions:

1. The laws of fluctuation in association within normal limits.

2. The direct effects of attention on the process of association, especially whether the validity of association relatively diminishes with the distance from the fixation point of consciousness.

A number of educated and uneducated persons were examined. A hundred stimulus words were given and the reactions noted. The reaction time was measured with a one fifth second stop watch. The second series consisted of one hundred associations plus internal distraction by means of the " A-phenomenon " (Cordes), and the third series of one hundred associations was taken by external distraction by means of a metronome. Altogether 12,400 associations were taken and were classified as follows:

I. Inner associations.
    1. Coördination; *e. g.,* cherry—apple, murder—gallows, sea—depth, father—God.
    2. Predicative relation; *e. g.,* snake—poisonous, war—bloody, mountain—beautiful, water—refreshing.
    3. Causal dependence; *e. g.,* cut—pain, pain—tears, appetite—fat, frost—cold.

[10] Jung und Riklin: Diagnost. Associationsstudien, Beit., I.

II. Outer associations.
    1. Coexistence; *e. g.,* ink—pen, pupil—teacher, Sunday —rest, table—chair.
    2. Identity; *e. g.,* beautiful—handsome, quarrel—**fight**.
    3. Speech—motor forms; *e. g.,* to suffer—hunger, to bow—head, to do—right, white—black.
III. Sound reactions.
    1. Word completion; *e. g.,* wonder—ful, friend— friendly.
    2. Sound; *e. g.,* blanket—blank, haircut—cut, longing— long, biting—fight.
    3. Rhyme; *e. g.,* nice—rice, ship—trip, never—clever, bone—stone.
IV. Remnant group.
    1. Mediate reactions; *e. g.,*

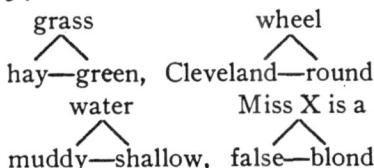

    2. Senseless reactions, where no words or associations are given.
    3. Failure = no reaction, and is due mostly to emotivity.
    4. Repeated stimulus word, another emotional phenomenon.
A. Perseveration, when reaction belongs to the preceding or following association.
B. Egocentric reaction; *e. g.,* rich—am I, young—am I.
C. Repetitions = repetition of content or style.
D. Speech combinations; *e. g.,* alliteration, same endings, etc.

On examining many associations it was found that the numerical relations in single individuals were quite fluctuating. The main reason for this, besides the individual ones, is the intensity of attention. The fact that certain individuals react by inner associations and others preferentially by outer associations is in the first place a phenomenon of attention. Every person endowed with speech has manifold qualities of associations at his disposal, the association quality uttered depending on the degree of attention evoked by the stimulus word. Whenever the distraction phenomena succeeded, the result was always the same, the outer associations and sound associations gained at the expense of the inner; that is, there was a deviation to the direction of the customary and smooth, hence to the automatically obvious, or habitual speech combination.

"Attention is a state characterized by muscular tension manifested in an association complex and furnishes the accentuated complex with the psycho-physical subsoil. The aim of the physical reflection seems to be the establishing of the toned presentation into consciousness. By the somatic connection the accentuated presentation is probably held on the height of distinctness in the stream of presentations. It becomes the 'directing' presentation (respectively the 'directing feeling') of the others. It causes two kinds of effects:

" 1. Promoting effects to all associated presentations and especially to all associated in the sense of direction.

" 2. Inhibiting effects to all presentations not associated, especially not associated in the sense of direction.

" If a non-associated presentation gains in attention, the directing presentation becomes correspondingly crowded from the fixation point, i. e., it loses in tone. The effects emanating from it likewise correspondingly lose in intensity and therefore the difference in the liminal value of all the others is diminished. The choice in the sense of direction becomes more difficult and is more and more subjected to the law of frequency, i. e., all those associations which through habit and practice form the most frequent content of consciousness push themselves forward. The law of frequency takes the place of the directing presentation. It means that the endeavor to conceive and elaborate the sense of the stimulus word is hindered by the interposition of presentations which are already blended and automatic in speech." Whenever there is a disturbance of attention we have to expect shallow reaction types or sound associations, and, conversely, whenever we get sound associations we have to presuppose a disturbance of attention.

COMPLEX-PHENOMENA AND THEIR CONSTELLATIONS.

By complex we mean the sum total of presentations connected with an emotionally accentuated event.

On examining the following associations, taken from an intel-ligent man of thirty-two, we note a number of peculiarities.

Stimulus.	Reaction.	Time.	Reproduction.
1. head	hair	1.6″	+
2. smooth	not	4.2″	love
3. to name	James	3.4″	no reaction
4. seeing	recently	3.2″	+
5. friendly	very	2.6″	+
6. wedding	never	4.0″	bells
7. to work	hard	2.8″	+
8. song	love	4.0″	+
9. green	hope	4.4″	grass
10. definite	certain	2.6″	+

The average reaction time in a person of his type is 2.4″; here we find quite a number above the average. We also note that some reactions are falsely reproduced, and in association 3 a failure of reproduction. Whenever such phenomena occur they are taken as complex-indicators. The stimulus word has either consciously or unconsciously touched a complex with strong affects. Here the reason for all this emotivity is readily explained by the fact that the test person was involved in an unfortunate love affair, and although the associations were taken years later the stimuli readily awakened the dormant complex. The associations were analyzed as follows: Association 2, smooth—not—love. Association 3, to name—James, means Jane, the name of his former fiancée. The test person was totally unconscious of this during the experiment, but on freely associating with the word James we got Jame—Jane. The subsequent associations were perseverations of the same complex. Association 4, seeing —recently, recalls the fact that the test person has recently seen his former fiancée. Association 5, friendly—very, is a description of their present mutual feelings. Association 6, wedding—never—bells, shows his definite decision. Associations 8 and 9, song—love and green—hope, belong to this same episode and are quite obvious without any further analysis.

We have here associations which are determined by definite constellations, inasmuch as they refer to an emotionally accentuated experience. These phenomena can be readily observed whenever associations are taken. Past experiences or complexes of strong feeling remain in the subconscious in a dormant state until they are disturbed by associations. These associations may be purely adventitious or intentional as in the experiment. As soon as stimulated they continue to manifest themselves in different automatisms. In the experiment we have definite responses which refer to the complex. In our everyday life we sometimes begin to hum a certain melody which we have not heard for years; for a time we become, as it were, possessed by it, and on analysis we find its definite meaning. It refers to some past episode evoked by some accidental association or by a definite state of mind.

" The preponderant part of all our thoughts and actions is really composed of small fragments which are infinitely and delicately determined by numberless moments lying entirely external to consciousness. To our ego-consciousness the association process seems to be its work, in its estimation the association process is dominated by the free will and attention, in reality, however, as is so nicely shown in the experiments, the ego-consciousness is only a marionette dancing on the stage by means of concealed automatic springs."[11]

Many assert that they can react of their free will and accord, but analysis shows that the reactions generally refer to their intimate experiences revealing just what they were endeavoring to conceal. The emotionally accentuated complex exerts a constant influence which successfully vies with the intentions of the ego-consciousness, and despite the repressing influences of the ego-complex it sends out associations about which the ego-complex has no notion.

The complexes as developed by Jung are identical with the dissociated psychic groups described by Freud. Just as the complexes dominate our thoughts and actions, so do the repressed psychic groups assert themselves symbolically not only in pathological but also in normal individuals. In his excellent work, the Psychopathologie des Alltagslebens,[12] Freud shows that everyday forgetfulness, lapses in writing, talking, adventitious acts and

[11] Jung: Diag. Associationsstudien, Beitr., IV.
[12] Freud: Zur Psychopathologie des Alltagslebens.

mistakes are nothing but the assertion of the split-off groups which, though repressed by the ego-consciousness, continue to manifest themselves on every possible occasion in the form of symbolic actions. The same is true of our dreams[13] where our repressed wishes are realized. It is impossible to give examples here, as they would be too long for the subject in hand.

These brief illustrations from the works of Freud and Jung give an intimation of the ideas expanded in this book. The author shows that just as in normal individuals and in hysteria the complex continues to play its part in dementia præcox, and as it does in dreams, the psychosis tends to actualize the repressed wishes from normal life. The otherwise known absurdities and incomprehensibilities become quite clear; every case has its special interests and its own individuality.

FREDERICK PETERSON,
A. A. BRILL.

NEW YORK, Jan., 1909.

[13] Freud: Die Traumdeutung.

AUTHOR'S PREFACE.

This work is the fruit of three years' experimental labor and clinical observation. In view of the difficulty and magnitude of the material, my work cannot and will not lay any claims either to perfection of treatment or to perfect certainty of conclusions and statements; on the contrary, it unites in itself all the disadvantages of eclecticism, which perhaps to many a reader will seem so peculiar that he will call my work rather a confession of faith than a scientific book.—*Peu importe!* What is of chief concern is that I may succeed in showing my readers how, by certain psychological investigations, I reached certain views, which I deem fit for the stimulation of the problems of the individual psychological basis of dementia præcox in a new and fruitful direction.

My views are no contrivances of a roving fancy, but thoughts which matured in almost daily intercourse with my venerable chief, Professor Bleuler. I owe special thanks to my friend, Dr. Riklin, of Rheinau, for considerably enriching my empirical material. Even a superficial glance at my work will show how indebted I am to the excellent conceptions of Freud. As Freud has not yet attained fair recognition and appreciation, but is opposed in the most authoritative circles, I hope to be allowed to define my position towards him. My attention was attracted to Freud by reading some of his articles, and indeed, at first accidentally by his " Traumdeutung," after which I studied also his other works. To be sure in the beginning I naturally entertained all the objections which are advanced in literature against Freud. However, I thought that Freud could only be refuted by one who himself had thoroughly tried the psychoanalytic method, and who should really investigate like Freud, that is, by studying out patiently and for a long time the daily life, hysteria and dreams from Freud's point of view. He who does not or cannot do this ought not to judge Freud, else he acts like those famous men of science who disdained to look through the telescope of Galileo.

Fairness to Freud does not signify, as many fear, a conditionless submission to a dogma; indeed independent judgment can very well be retained beside it. If I, for instance, recognize the complex mechanisms of dreams and hysteria, it does not at all mean that I ascribe to sexual trauma in youth an exclusive significance, as Freud apparently does; still less does it mean that I place sexuality so preponderantly in the foreground, or that I even ascribe to it the psychological universality which Freud postulates under the impression of the very powerful rôle which sexuality plays in the psyche. As for Freud's therapy, it is at best a possible one, and perhaps does not always come up to expectations. Nevertheless, all these are only side issues which completely disappear beside the psychological principles, the discovery of which is Freud's greatest reward, and to which the critic does not pay enough attention. He who wishes to be fair to Freud should act in accordance with the words of Erasmus: *Unumquemque move lapidem, omnia experire nihil intentatum relinque.*

As my work is often based on experimental examinations, I hope that the reader will pardon me if he finds many references to the " Diagnostischen Associations-Studien."[1]

C. G. JUNG.

ZURICH, July, 1906.
[1] J. A. Barth, Leipzig, 1906.

CHAPTER I.

CRITICAL PRESENTATION OF THEORETICAL VIEWS ON THE PSYCHOLOGY OF DEMENTIA PRÆCOX.

The interpretation of the psychological disturbances of dementia præcox are found in literature only in the form of fragmentary attempts which although they at times go quite far, yet nowhere have they any clear coördination. The statements of the older authors have only a limited value as they refer now to this now to that form of mental disease which can only be indefinitely classified as dementia præcox. Hence one must not attribute to them any general validity. The first general view concerning the nature of the psychological disturbance in catatonia was that of Tschisch,[1] who, in 1886, thought that it was essentially due to inability of attention. A similar but somewhat differently conceived view was given by Freusberg.[2] He stated that the automatic actions of the catatonic are associated with a condition of reduction of consciousness which causes a loss of control over his psychical processes. The motor disturbances are only symptomatic expressions for the degree of psychic tension.

According to Freusberg the motor catatonic symptoms are dependent upon corresponding psychological manifestations. The "weakening of consciousness" points to the quite modern view of Pierre Janet. Also Kraepelin,[3] Aschaffenburg,[4] Ziehen and others affirm that there is a disturbance of attention. In 1894 we meet for the first time with an experimental psychological work on the subject of catatonia. It is the investigation of Sommer, "On the Study of 'Inhibition' of Mental Processes."[5]

The author makes the following statements which are of gen-

---

[1] Cited from Ehrich Arndt: Uber die Geschichte der Katatonie, Zentr.-f. Nervenheilk. u. Psych., Bd. XIV, p. 81.
[2] Freusberg, 1886, Archiv f. Psych., XVII, p. 758.
[3] Lehrbuch d. Psychiatrie.
[4] Allg. Ztschr. f. Psych., 1898.
[5] Allg. Ztschr. f. Psych., Bd. L.

eral significance: (1) The course of ideation is retarded. (2) The attention of the patient is frequently so fixed by pictures shown him that he can only with difficulty rid himself of them.

The frequent obstructions (the retardations of reaction time) are explained by Sommer by the visual fixation.[6] The condition of absent-mindedness among normal persons occasionally shows similar phenomena; e. g., amazement and " staring into vacancy." Because of this analogy of the catatonic condition to normal absent-mindedness Sommer affirms something similar to Tschisch and Freusberg, namely, that there is a diminution of attention. Catalepsy according to Sommer is another phenomenon closely related to optical fixation and which he considers " in all cases as a phenomenon of thoroughly psychic origin." With this conception Sommer places himself in sharp contrast to the view of Roller, to which also Clemens Neisser unconditionally adheres.

Says Roller: " The presentations and sensations which among the insane chiefly come to perception, forcing themselves into the field of consciousness, are those which have been caused by the morbid states of the subordinate centers, and when active apperception, the attention, enters into activity it becomes fixed and held by the morbid perceptions," etc.[7]

By way of addition Neisser observes: " Wherever we look in insanity we always meet with something strange which cannot be explained according to the analogy of normal psychical activity. The logical mechanisms in insanity are put in motion not through the apperceptive or associative conscious psychic activity, but by pathological irritations lying under the threshold of consciousness."[8] Neisser therefore agrees with the concepts of Roller. This view does not seem to me to be without its objections. Firstly, it is based upon an anatomical conception of the psychic processes, a view against which too much warning cannot be given. What part the " subordinate centers " play in the origin

[6] v. Leupold, who recently elaborated this symptom, names this manifestation " das Symptom der Benennung u. des Abtastens " (the symptom of naming and touching). Zur Symptomatologie der Katatonie. Klinik für psychische u. nervöse Krankheiten, Vol. I, H. I.

[7] Cited from Neisser's, Über die Katatonie. Stuttgart-Enke, 1887, p. 61.

[8] Ernst Meyer, too, leans towards this view which was then also held by Kraepelin.—E. Meyer: Beitrage zur Kenntnis der acut entstandenen Psychosen. Habilitationsschrift. Berlin, 1899.

of the psychic elements, such as presentations, feelings, etc., we do not know at all. An explanation of this kind rests merely upon words.

Secondly, the Roller-Neisser view seems to presuppose that beyond consciousness the whole psyche ceases. From the French psychology and from experiences with hypnotism we learn that this is not the case.

Thirdly, if I understand correctly, by " pathological irritations lying under the threshold of consciousness " Neisser means cell processes in the cortex. This hypothesis goes too far. All psychic processes are correlates of cell processes, as well according to materialistic conceptions as according to the doctrine of psycho-physical parallelism. It is therefore not singular that psychic processes in catatonia should be correlates of a corresponding physical series. We know that normal psychical processes originate under the constant influence of numerous psychological constellations which as a rule are unknown to us. Why should this fundamental psychological law suddenly vanish in catatonia? Is it because the ideational content of the catatonic is foreign to his consciousness? Is it not the same with our dreams? And yet no one will assert that dreams originate so to speak directly from the cells without psychological constellations. Whoever has analyzed dreams according to the method of Freud knows what an enormous influence the constellations have. The appearance of strange ideas in consciousness without any demonstrable connections with former contents of consciousness is not an unheard of thing in either the psychology of the normal or the hysteric. The " pathological fancies " of catatonics have rich analogies in the normal and in hysterics (see further). What we lack is not so much comparative material but the key to open the psychology of the catatonic automatism. It seems to me in general rather daring to assume something *toto cœlo* new and absolutely foreign in natural science.

In dementia præcox, where numberless normal associations actually still exist, we must expect that until we shall learn to know those very fine processes which are really specific, the laws of the normal psyche will long continue to be manifest. Unfortunately to the great detriment of psychopathology, in which we are just beginning to agree upon our misunderstandings of conceptions applied, our knowledge of the normal psyche is still on a very primitive basis.

We are grateful to Sommer[9] for further fruitful studies of the associations in catatonia.

In certain cases of catatonia[10] the associations flow in a normal manner only to be suddenly interrupted by an apparently totally disconnected, peculiarly-mannered connection of ideas, as will be seen by the following example: dark—green, white—brown, black—" good day, William," red—brown.

These saltatory associations were also confirmed by Diem,[11] who conceives them as sudden " fancies." Sommer justly considers them as an important criterion of catatonia. The " pathological inspirations " as described by Breukink,[12] who follows Ziehen, can be readily found in every insane asylum where these authors have observed them. They are exclusively seen in dementia præcox, and especially play an important rôle in the paranoid types. Bonhoeffer's[13] " pathological fancies " probably refer to the same manifestations. The problem instigated by the discovery of Sommer is by no means settled, but until we become more enlightened we are obliged to group under the same heading the phenomena observed by various authors which are nearly all designated by almost the same name. Although from clinical experience it would seem that " pathological fancies " appear only in the realm of dementia præcox, naturally excluding the falsifications of memory which often suddenly appear in organic dementia and in Korsakow's symptom-complex, I wish to observe that in the realm of hysteria, principally in cases that never seek the asylum, " pathological fancies " often play a great part. Flournoy[14] reports the most interesting examples. Similar sud-

[9] Lehrbuch der Psychopathologischen Untersuchungsmethoden, 1899.

[10] Sommer: Lehrbuch, p. 362. Recently Fuhrmann has made some association experiments in " acute juvenile dementia " without any characteristic results. Arch. f. Psych., Vol. XL, p. 817.

[11] Diem: Die einfach demente Form der Dementia Præcox (Dementia simplex). Arch. f. Psych., Vol. XXXVII.

[12] Breukink: Uber eknoische Zustände. Monatsschr. f. Psych. u. Neur., Vol. XIV.

[13] Deutsche med. Wochenschrift, No. 39, 1904.

[14] Flournoy: Des Indes à la planète Mars. Etude sur un cas de Somnambulisme avec glossolalie. Paris et Genève, 1900.—III Nouvelles obser-

den invasions of changed psychological activity I observed in a very clear case of hysteria,[15] and recently I could again confirm it in a similar case. Finally, as I have shown, sudden disturbances of association by the incursion of seemingly strange connections of ideas also appear in the normal.[16] In the saltatory association or " pathological fancy " we are perhaps dealing with a widely disseminated psychical phenomenon, and without further discussion we can agree with Sommer that the most marked type appears in dementia præcox.

Sommer, in examining the associations of catatonics, found numerous sound associations and stereotypies. By stereotypies we mean frequent repetitions of former reactions. In our examinations we simply name it " repetitions." The reaction time showed enormous fluctuations.

In 1902 Ragnar Vogt[17] again took up the problem of the catatonic consciousness. He proceeded from the Müller-Pilzecker investigations[18] by considering mainly their observations about " perseveration." The continuation of psychic processes or their correlates, even after being replaced in consciousness by other ideas, is according to Vogt the normal analogy to catatonic perseveration, such as verbigeration, catalepsy, etc. Accordingly, in catatonia the tendency to perseveration of the psychophysical functions would be especially marked. But inasmuch as in the Müller-Pilzecker observations perseveration is manifested most distinctly only when no new content of consciousness impresses itself,[19] Vogt claims that in catatonia perse-

vations sur un cas de somnambulisme avec glossolalie. Archives de Psychologie de la Suisse Romande, T. I, p. 102.

[15] Zur Psychologie und Pathologie sogenannter occulter Phänomene. Leipzig, 1902.

[16] Diagnostische Assoz. Stud., IV Beitrag. Über das Verhalten der Reaktionszeit beim Assoziationsexperiment. J. A. Barth, Leipzig, 1906.

[17] R. Vogt: Zur Psychologie der Katatonischen Symptome. Zentr. f. Nervenheilk. u. Psych., Bd. XIX, p. 433.

[18] Zeitschrift für Psych. u. Phys. der Sinnesorgane, Erg. B. I, 1901.

[19] In conditions of distraction there is an increase of preseveration in the association experiments. See Diag. Assoz. Stud., I Beitrag, and interesting experiments of Stransky: Über Sprachverwirrtheit, 1905. Marhold, Halle. See also the excellent work of Heilbronner: Über Haftenbleiben und Stereotypie (Monatsschr. f. Psych. u. Neur., Bd. XVIII, Erg.-Heft), which accepts similar theoretical views.

veration is only possible because no other interesting conscious process occurs. Hence it must be assumed that there is a certain narrowing of consciousness. From this we can also understand the resemblance between the hypnotic and the catatonic states.[20] The impulsive acts of catatonia are likewise explained by the narrowing of consciousness, thus preventing the intervention of any inhibition. Vogt is apparently under the influence of Pierre Janet, to whom the " narrowing of consciousness " and diminution of attention is the same as *abaissement du niveau mental*.[21] Here then we again meet the already mentioned view, though in a somewhat more modern and generalized form, namely, that in catatonia there is a disturbance of attention, or as I prefer to express it in a more general term, there is a disturbance of positive psychic function.[22] The reference to the similarity of hypnotic conditions is very interesting, but unfortunately Vogt gave us only a mere outline.

Kindred views are advanced by Evensen.[23] He draws a skilful parallel between catatonia and absent-mindedness. Lack of ideas in a narrowed consciousness is the foundation of catalepsy, etc.

A painstaking and detailed examination of the psychology of catatonia is the thesis of René Masselon.[24] The author first affirms that diminution of attention (distraction perpétuelle) is the main characteristic. He conceives attention in a very general and comprehensive sense corresponding to his French training in psychology. He says, " The perception of external objects, the perception of our own personality, judgment, the ideas of rela-

[20] I call attention here to the work of Kaiser: Differentialdiagnose zwischen Hysterie und Katatonie. Allgem. Ztschr. f. Psych., LVIII.

[21] P. Janet: Les Obsessions et la Psychasthénie. Paris, 1903. Janet presents similar views in his earlier works: Névroses et Idées Fixes, and Automatisme Psychologique.

[22] According to Binet attention is "a mental adaptation to a state which is new for us." Attention et Adaptation. Année Psychologique, 1900.

[23] Die psychologische Grundlage der Katatonischen Krankheitszeichen. Zentralbl. für Neurol. Psych., etc. Edited by v. S. Kure and K. Miura, Tokio, Bd. II.

[24] Masselon: Psychologie des Déments Précoces. Thèse de Paris, 1902. (The work of Masselon " La Démence Précoce " is rather a clinical compendium of the disease.)

tionship, faith and certitude disappear when the power of attention disappears."

As shown by this citation, much depends on attention as conceived by Masselon. The more general features of the catatonic
condition he summarizes as "*apathie, aboulie, perte de l'activité
intellectuelle.*" A brief consideration of these three abstractions
teaches that fundamentally they mean the same thing, and indeed,
Masselon in his work always tries to find that word or simile
which would best express the innermost essence of his correct
feeling. However, scarcely any concept of human language
should be so broad; indeed, there is no one who has not already
been impressed by some school or system with the biased limits
of meaning. We can best find out what Masselon conceives as
the essence of dementia præcox by listening to the wording of
some of his statements: "The habitual state is the emotional
apathy . . . these disturbances are intimately connected with the
disturbances of intelligence: they are of the same nature . . .
the patients do not manifest any desires . . . all volition is destroyed . . . the disappearance of desire is connected with
all the other disturbances of mental activity . . . a veritable
weakness of cerebral activity . . . the elements of the mind
show a tendency to live an individual life not being any more
systematized by the inactive mind."[25]

In Masselon's work there is a mixture of many things and
views that he feels belong to one root which, however, he is
unable to find without obscuring his work. Nevertheless, in
spite of his shortcomings, Masselon's researches contain useful
observations. Thus he finds a striking resemblance between
dementia præcox and hysteria in the marked self-distractibility
of the patient by everything possible and especially by his own
symptoms (Sommer's optical fixation), and also in exhaustibility
and capricious memory. German critics have reproached him
for this discovery, but certainly unjustly when we consider that
Masselon means only the reproductive ability. If a patient gives
a wrong answer to a direct question it is taken by the German
school as by-speaking (Vorbeireden) as negativism; in other
words, as active resistance. Masselon, however, considers this
as an inability to reproduce. When superficially considered it

[25] Masselon: *l. c.*, p. 62, 71, 135, 140.

may mean both, the divergence being due to different interpretations bestowed upon this phenomenon. Masselon speaks of a "*véritable obscurcissment de l'image-souvenir,*" he considers the disturbances of memory as "*la disparition de la conscience de certains souvenirs, et l'incapacité du malade à les retrouver.*" The contradiction of both conceptions becomes clear without further explanation when one thinks of the psychology of hysteria. When a hysterical patient replies during the anamnesis " I do not know, I have forgotten," it simply means " I cannot or will not say it, for it is something very unpleasant."[26] Very often the " I don't know " is so awkward that the reason for not knowing is quite obvious. I have given many experimental proofs to show that the defects occurring in the association experiments, such as want of reaction, have the same psychology.[27] It is often only with difficulty that one can decide whether hysterics really do not know or whether they merely cannot or will not answer. Those who are in the habit of examining cases of dementia præcox in a somewhat detailed manner realize what exertion is often necessary to obtain the proper information. Sometimes one is certain that the patients know it, again it is an obstruction (Sperrung) which makes quite an involuntary impression upon one, and finally there are cases in which one is obliged to talk about an " amnesia " just as in hysteria, where from amnesia to unwillingness to talk is only a step. Finally the association experiment shows us that these phenomena exist in the normal person, though only *in nuce.*[28] According to Masselon the disturbances of memory and attention originate from the same source, though it is not clear from what source. In contrast to this the author finds ideas that obstinately persist, which he qualifies as follows: " Certain memories which were formerly more intimately connected with the effective personality of the patient tend to reproduce themselves incessantly and

[26] See the works of Freud, also Riklin: Zur Psychologie hysterischer Dämmerzustände und des Ganserschen Symptoms. Psych.-neur. Wochenschr., 1906.
[27] Diagnost. Assoz. Stud., IV Beitrag. Über das Verhalten der Reaktionszeit beim Assoziationsexperiment u. Experimentelle Beobachtungen über das Erinnerungsvermögen. Zentr.-Bl. f. Nervenheilk. u. Psych., Jahrgang XXVIII, p. 653.
[28] Cf. Diagnost. Assoz. Stud., IV Beitrag.

to continually occupy consciousness . . . the persisting memories assume a stereotyped form . . . thought tends to become clotted ('gerinnen ')."[20]   Without attempting to produce further proof Masselon declares that the stereotyped ideas (delusions) are associations of the complex of personality. It is a pity that the author does not linger any longer on this point. It would be very interesting to know in what way, for example, a few neologisms or a "word salad" are associations of the complex of personality, as indeed these are often the only remnants through which we become informed of the existence of ideas. That the psychic life of the adolescent dement "curdles" or "clots" seems to me an excellent simile for the gradual torpescence of the disease; it designates quite pregnantly the impressions entertained by every careful observer of dementia præcox. The author found it quite easy to derive automatism (*suggestibilité*) from his premises. As to the origin of negativism he offers but vague suppositions, although the French literature on impulsive phenomena afforded him many essential facts for analogous explanations. Masselon also tried association experiments. He found many repetitions of the stimulus words and frequent fancies of an apparently quite fortuitous nature. From these experiments he concluded that the patients are unable to pay attention. A right conclusion! Masselon, however, spent too little time on the "fancies."

From the main results of Masselon's work it can be seen that this author, like his predecessors, is inclined to admit a true central psychological disturbance,[30] a disturbance which sets in at the source of life of all psychic functions; that is, in the realms of apperception, feeling and desire.[31]

Weygandt in his clear elucidation of the psychology of the weak-mindedness in dementia præcox follows Wundt's terminology and calls the terminal process of the disease apperceptive

[20] Masselon: *l. c.*, p. 69, 261, 263.

[30] Séglas (Leçons cliniques), 1895, says the following about the uncertainty of catatonic accomplishments: There is nothing surprising when one reflects that all movement requires the previous synthesis of a crowd of mental representations—and it is precisely the power to make this mental synthesis which is defective in these individuals.

[31] Kant: Kritik der praktischen Vernunft.

dementia.[32]   It is well known that Wundt's conception of apperception is a most general one.   It embraces not only the Binet and Masselon conception of attention, but also Janet's idea of the " fonction du réel."[33]   But we shall return to this.   To show the universality of the apperception idea in the sense indicated I shall quote Wundt's own words: " The condition characterized by peculiar feelings which accompanies the clearer reception of a psychic content we call attention, the single process by which any psychic content is brought to clear conception is apperception.[34]   The apparent antithesis between attention and apperception is solved as follows: " Accordingly, attention and apperception are expressions for one and the same psychological fact. The first of these expressions we choose by preference for the ' subjective ' side of this fact to express the accompanying feelings and sensations; by means of the second we designate mainly the ' objective ' results, the alterations in the quality of the contents of consciousness."[35]

In the definition: apperception is the " single process by means of which any psychic content is brought to clear conception," much is said in few words.   According to this definition apperception is will, sensation, affect, suggestion, impulsive phenomena, etc., because all these are processes by means of which " a psychic content is brought to clear conception."   We do not attempt to give an unfavorable criticism on the apperceptive idea, but merely to indicate its enormous extent.   It embraces every positive psychic function, especially the progressive acquisition of new associations; that is, no more and no less than all enigmas of physical activity both conscious and unconscious. Weygandt's idea, therefore, of apperceptive dementia expresses that which Masselon dimly felt.   Nevertheless, in this we find only a general expression for the psychology of dementia præcox. It is too general to be of any force in the deduction of all symptoms.

[32] W. Weygandt: Alte Dementia Præcox. Zentr.-Bl. f. Nervenheilk. u. Psych., Jahrgang XXVII, p. 613.

[33] Obsessions et Psychasthénie, Vol. I, p. 433.   The *fonction du réel* can also be expressed in other words as psychological adaptation to the environment or acting up to reality.   It corresponds to the "adaptation" of Binet, which represents a special side of apperception.

[34] Gundriss der Psychologie, 1902, p. 249.

[35] Grundzüge der Physiol. Psychologie, 1903, p. 341.

Madeleine Pelletier[36] examines in her thesis associations in manic flight of ideas, and in mental debility. By mental debility we understand typical cases of dementia præcox. The theoretic standpoint from which this author considers flight of ideas agrees in its essentials with that of Liepmann.[37] A knowledge of Liepmann's work is presupposed.

Pelletier compares the shallow flow of associations in dementia præcox to the flight of ideas. The characteristic of flight of ideas is "*absence du principe directeur*" (absence of directing principle). The same takes place in the course of the associations in dementia præcox. "The directing idea is absent and the state of consciousness remains vague without any ordering of its elements." The only state of normal psychic activity which can be compared to mania is revery, yet revery may rather be a weak-minded than a maniacal mode of thinking. Pelletier is right in finding a great similarity between normal revery and the shallow associations of maniacs, but only when the associations are written on paper. Clinically the manic does not by any means look like a dreamer. The author evidently feels this and finds the analogy rather more fitting for dementia præcox, which condition has been compared to that of dreams since the times of Reil (*e. g.,* Chaslin: "La confusion mentale primitive"). The richness and acceleration of presentations in manic flight of ideas differentiates it sharply from the very stagnant slowly-coursing association type of dreams and especially from the poverty and numberless perseverations in the associations of catatonics. The analogy is correct only in so far as concerns the directing idea which is absent in both of these cases; in mania because all presentations crowd themselves into consciousness with marked acceleration and with strong feeling tones,[38] there-

---

[36] L'Association des idées dans la manie aigue et dans la débilité mentale. Thèse de Paris, 1903.

[37] Liepmann: Über Ideenflucht, Begriffsbestimmung u. psychologische Analyse. Halle, 1904.

[38] It is true that Aschaffenburg found a certain prolongation of the association time in manic cases. It should, however, not be forgotten that in acoustic-speech experiments attention and speech expression play a great rôle. One observes or measures expression of speech only, and not connections of ideas.

fore no attention can probably take place,[39] and in revery there is no attention to begin with, and where this is lacking the flow of associations must sink into revery. According to the laws of association there results a slowly progressive course, tending principally towards likeness, contrast, coexistence and motor-speech combinations.[40] Numerous examples can be observed daily by attentively following a general conversation. As Pelletier shows, the course of association in dementia præcox is constructed upon a similar scheme. This can best be seen by an example:

" Je suis l'être, l'être ancien, le vieil Hêtre,[41] que l'on peut écrire avec un H. Je suis universel, primordial, divine, catholique, Romaine,[32] l'eusses-tu cru, l'être tout cru, suprumu,[43] l'enfant Jésus.[44] Je m'appelle Paul, c'est un nom, ce n'est pas une négation,[45] on en connait la signification.[46] . . . Je suis éternel, immense, il n'y a ni haut, ni bas, fluctuat nec mergitur, le petit bâteau,[47] vous n'avez pas peur de tomber."[48]

This example shows us very distinctly the type of association in dementia præcox. It is a very shallow one and carries many sound associations. Yet the disintegration is so marked that we cannot compare it to the reveries of the normal state, but are obliged to compare it to dreams. Only in dreams is such speech observed.[49] Rich examples can be found in Freud's " Die Traumdeutung."

In the first contribution of the " Diagnostische Associationsstudien " it was proven that diminished attention produced shallow association types, motor-speech combinations, sound associations, etc., and inversely, the appearance of shallow associa-

[39] Acceleration and emotional strength of ideas are at least that which we can verify by observation. This, however, does in no way exclude the fact that there are other essential moments to consider which are, at present, inaccessible to our cognition.
[40] Diagnost. Associationsstudien, I Beitrag, Einleitung.
[41] Assonance.   [42] Contiguité.
[43] Assonance.   [44] Assonance.
[45] Assonance.   [46] Assonance.
[47] Resemblance and contiguity, immense suggested to him the ocean, then the bâteau and the aphorism which forms the shield of the city of Paris.
[48] Pelletier: l. c., p. 142.
[49] Kraepelin: Arch. f. Psych., Vol. XXVI, p. 595, and Stransky: Über Sprachverwirrtheit, 1905, point out the same thing.

tion types always pointed to a disturbance of attention. According to our experimental proofs Pelletier is right when she refers to the shallow types of dementia præcox as the result of lowered attention. She calls this diminution by the words of Janet, *"abaissement du niveau mental."* From this work, too, it can be seen that the disturbance is again taken back to the central problem of apperception.

It is to be noted that the author overlooks the perseverations, but on the other hand we are grateful to her for the valuable observation on symbolism and symbolic relations so very frequent in dementia præcox. She says: " It is to be remarked that the symbol plays a very great part in the discursions of the insane. It is encountered everywhere among the persecuted and weak-minded. It is a very inferior form of thought. The symbol could be defined as a false perception of a relation of identity or a very marked analogy between two objects which in reality present only a very vague analogy."[50]

This quotation shows that Pelletier brings the catatonic symbols into relation with disordered attention. This supposition is decidedly supported by the fact that the symbol has since long been known as a usual manifestation in revery and dreams.

The psychology of negativism, concerning which numerous publications already exist, forms a separate chapter. The symptom of negativism certainly ought not to be considered as something definite. There are many forms and grades of negativism which have not as yet been clinically studied and analyzed with the necessary accuracy. The division of negativism into active and passive forms can be easily understood. The most complicated psychological cases appear under the form of active resistance. If an analysis were possible in those cases, it would frequently be found that very definite motives exist for the resistance, and it would then be doubtful if one could still talk of negativism. In the passive form, too, there are many cases which are difficult to interpret. Notwithstanding this there are numerous cases in which one may clearly point out that even simple processes of volition are always blindly converted into their opposite. According to our view negativism always ultimately depends on corresponding associations. Whether there

[50] Pelletier: *l. c.,* p. 129.

is a negativism taking place in the spinal cord I do not know. The most general standpoint on the question of negativism is taken by Bleuler in his work on negative suggestibility.[51] He shows that negative suggestibility, that is, the impulse toward contrast associations, is not only a constituent part of the normal psyche, but also a frequent mechanism of pathological symptoms in hysteria, impulsive phenomena, and dementia præcox. The contrast mechanism is an independent function entirely rooted in " affectivity." It therefore manifests itself mainly in presentations of strong feeling as in decisions and similar things. " This mechanism protects against a rash act and forces the consideration of, for and against." The contrast mechanism is a counterpart of suggestibility. Suggestibility is the faculty of the reception and realization of strong feeling-toned ideas, while the contrast mechanism guards the opposite. It is for this reason that Bleuler appropriately calls it negative suggestibility. The fact that these two functions are so closely related readily explains why they are met with together clinically. In hysteria we have suggestibility near insuperable contrary autosuggestion; and negativism, automatism and echopraxy in dementia præcox, etc.

The importance of negative suggestibility in every-day psychical occurrences explains why contrast associations are everywhere enormously frequent. They are in the closest relationship.[52]

In language, too, we see something similar. The words which express the usual contrasts are very closely associated and therefore mostly belong to the intimate associations of language, as, white, black, etc. In primitive languages one occasionally finds only one word for contrasting ideas. According to Bleuler a

[51] Bleuler: Die negative Suggestibilität ein psychologisches Prototyp des Negativismus, der conträren Autosuggestion und gewisser Zwangsideen. Psych.-Neurol. Wochenschr., 1904.
[52] The following express themselves in a similar manner: Paulhan: L'activité mentale et les elements de l'esprit, 1889.—Svenson: Om Katatonie. Hygiea, 1902.—Janet: Les Obsessions, 1903.—Pick: On Contrary Actions. Journal of Nervous and Mental Disease, Jan., 1904.—An instructive case is given by Josiah Royce: The Case of John Bunyon. Psychological Review, 1894, p. 143. [Jelliffe: Pre Dementia Præcox, Am. Jour. Med. Sc. 1907. Ed.]

relatively mild emotional disturbance will suffice to produce nega-tivistic phenomena. Janet ("Les Obsessions," Vol. I, p. 60) shows that in persons suffering from impulsive ideas, the "*abais-sement du niveau mental*" suffices to liberate a play of contrasts. What, therefore, can we expect from the " apperceptive demen-tia " in dementia præcox! Indeed, here we really find the appar-ently irregular play of positive and negative which is very often nicely reflected in the associations as expressed in speech.[53] Hence in the problem of negativism we have sufficient evidence that this symptom too, is in close relationship with "appercep-tive dementia." The central control of the psyche is so weak-ened that it can neither further the positive nor inhibit the nega-tive acts, or the reverse may be true.[54]

Let us now recapitulate what has been said. The authors thus far mentioned have essentially affirmed that diminution of atten-tion, or more generally speaking, " apperceptive dementia " (Weygandt) is characteristic of dementia præcox. The exist-ence of the peculiar shallowing of the associations, symbolisms, stereotypies, perseverations, command automatism, apathy, abou-lia, disturbances of reproduction, and, in a limited sense, nega-tivism, are all due to apperceptive dementia.

That neither apprehension nor retention take part as a rule in the general deterioration, seems at first sight rather singular. As a matter of fact one can find in dementia præcox during acces-sible moments that there exists a surprisingly good, and an almost photographic memory, which preferably takes note of the most indifferent things that unfailingly escape the notice of normal persons.[55] But just such peculiarity shows what the nature of memory is. It is nothing but a passive registration of events which take place in the nearest surroundings. But all that which requires an effort of attention passes without heed by the patient, or at most it is registered *à niveau* together with the daily visits of the doctor and dinner; at least so it appears to us. Weygandt (*l. c.*) very nicely describes this lack of active acquisition. Ap-

---

[53] Compare the analyses of Pelletier, *l. c.*, as well as the experimental examinations of Stransky: Über Sprachverwirrtheit.

[54] Further works on negativism have already been criticised by Bleuler: *l. c.*

[55] Kraepelin, too, is of the opinion that the apprehension is not more intensively damaged; it is only an increased inclination to an arbitrary pro-duction of incoming ideas. Lehrbuch, VII Aufl., p. 177.

prehension is generally disturbed only during periods of excite-ment. Apprehension and retention, or impressibility and reten-tiveness, are for the most part only passive processes which take place in us without the expenditure of a great amount of energy, just as mere hearing and seeing when unaccompanied by attention.

From Weygandt's idea of " apperceptive dementia " (Janet—*abaissement du niveau mental*) one can in a measure deduce the origin of the above mentioned symptoms (automatism, stereo-typy, etc.) ; but we are unable from this to understand the indi-vidual multiformity of the symptoms, their capriciousness, the peculiar content of the delusions, hallucinations, etc. Many investigators have already attempted to solve this riddle.

Stransky[56] examined dementia præcox from the clinical point of view. Proceeding from Kraepelin's idea of " emotional de-mentia," he asserts that by this conception two things are under-stood. Firstly, poverty or superficiality of emotional reactions, secondly an incoördination between the same and the content of consciousness dominating the psyche.[57]   In this fashion Stransky differentiates the content of Kraepelin's idea, showing that clin-ically one sees more than the " emotional dementia." The strik-ing incongruity between idea and affect which we can daily observe in dementia præcox, is a more frequent symptom during the development of the disease than the emotional demen-tia. The incongruity between idea and emotional tone forced Stransky to accept two separate psychical factors, the noöpsyche and the thymopsyche. The former idea embraces all pure intel-lectual, the latter the affective processes. Both these ideas nearly correspond in Schopenhauer's psychology to intellect and will. In the healthy psyche there is naturally a constant, very fine, simultaneous, coördinated action of both factors. But as soon as incoördination steps in, it corresponds analogically to ataxia, and we then have the picture of dementia præcox with all its disproportionate and unintelligible affects. So far the

[56] Stransky: Zur Kenntniss gewisser erworbener Blödsinnsformen, 1903. Jahrb. f. Psych., Vol. XXIV, p. 1.

[57] Jahrbuch. f. Psych., XXIV, p. 28.—Idem: Zur Lehre von der Dementia præcox. Zentr.-Bl. f. Nervenheilk. u. Psych., XXII Jahrg.—Idem: Zur Auffassung gewisser symptome der Dementia præcox. Neurol. Zentr.-Bl., 1904, Nr. 23, u. 24.—Idem: Über die Dementia præcox. Wiener mediz. Presse, 1905.

divisions of the psychic functions into noö- and thymopsychic agree with reality. But it is a question whether a trite content of consciousness manifested in the patient with an enormous affect seems incongruous only to us who can only most sparingly look into his soul, or is it the same for the subjective sensation of the patient. I shall make myself clear by the following example:

I visit a gentleman in his office. Suddenly he starts up enraged and swears most excitedly at a clerk who placed a newspaper on the right instead of the left side of the table. I am astonished and make a mental note about the peculiar nervousness of this person. But after a while I learn from the other employees that the clerk has done the same thing wrongly dozens of times and hence the anger of the man was quite adequate.

Had I not received subsequent explanations I should have formed a wrong picture of the psychology of this person. We are frequently confronted with a similar condition in dementia præcox. Owing to the peculiar seclusiveness of the patients we see into them but little, a fact which every psychiatrist will substantiate. It is therefore readily understood that many excitements appear to us inexplicable because we do not see their associate causes. That may even happen to us. We are occasionally for a time in bad humor, and quite inadequately so without being conscious of its cause. The simplest responses are then uttered in a disproportionate, emphatic, and irritable tone, etc. If even a normal individual is not always clear about the causes of his ill-humor, how little can we know when confronted with the mind of a precocious dement? On account of the evident inadequacy of our psychological diagnosis, we must be very careful about the supposition of a real incoördination in the sense of Stransky. Although judging from clinical appearances there are frequent incongruities, they are by no means exclusively limited to dementia præcox. In hysteria, likewise, the incongruity is an every-day occurrence. One can see it in the very trite fact of the so-called hysterical " exaggerations," whose counterpart is the well known *" belle indifférence "* of hysterics. We also find violent excitements over nothing, at times over something which in no way shows any recognizable connection with the excitement. Yet psycho-analysis uncovers the motives, and we then begin to understand why the patients reacted in such a manner. In dementia præcox we are at present unable to penetrate deep enough so that the relations remain unknown, and we therefore assume an "ataxia" between noö- and thymo-psyche. Thanks to analysis we know that in hysteria there is no "ataxia," but only an oversensitiveness, which, as soon as we know the pathogenic ideational complex, becomes clear and intelligible.[58] Knowing how the incongruity is brought about in hysteria, is it still necessary that we should accept a totally new mechanism in dementia præcox? In general we know by far too little about the psychology of the normal and hysteric[59] to dare to accept in such an untransparent disease as dementia præcox, a totally new mechanism unknown to all psychology. One should be economical with new principles of interpretation. It is for this reason that I repudiate the clear and ingenious hypothesis of Stransky. As a compensation for the above, we possess a very excellent experimental work by Stransky[60] which gives us the foundation for the understanding of an important symptom, namely, the speech disorders.

The speech disorder is the product of the main psychological disturbance. Stransky calls it "intrapsychic ataxia." Whenever there is a disturbance at the points of contact of the emotional life and ideation, as in dementia præcox, producing thereby in the normal thought the lack of orientation by a controlling idea (Liepmann), there must result a stream of thought resembling flight of ideas. As Pelletier has shown, the laws of association predominate against the influence of direction. If it is a question of a process of speech there must result an increase in the purely superficial elements of connection (motor speech association and sound reactions), as was shown in our associa-

---

[58] An hysterical woman, for example, one day merged into a deep and persistent depression "because the weather is so dull and rainy." The analysis, however, showed that the depression set in on the anniversary of a very sad and important event in the life of the patient.

[59] Binet (Les altérations de la personnalité, p. 89) approximately remarks: Hysterics are for us only subjects of choice, exaggerating phenomena that one must necessarily find in some degree among a crowd of other persons who are not at all tainted, even slightly, by the hysterical neurosis.

[60] Stransky: Über Sprachverwirrtheit.

tion experiments with distracted attention.   Hand in hand with this there is a diminution of sensory connections.   Besides these many other disturbances show themselves, such as an increase of the mediate associations, the senseless reactions, and frequent repetitions of the stimulus words.   Perseverations show a most contradictory behavior during distractibility.   According to our experiments they are increased in women and decreased in men. In a great many cases we could explain the resulting persevera- tions by the presence of a strong feeling tone.   Every-day expe- rience teaches us that a strong feeling-toned idea shows a special tendency to perseverate.   By distracting the attention there results a certain emptiness of consciousness[61] in which ideas can more easily perseverate than during complete attention.

Stransky then studied the results of continuous speech asso- ciation under the influence of relaxed attention.   His test per- sons had to talk at random into a phonograph for one minute on anything or in any way they chose.   At the same time they were not to pay attention to what they said.   A stimulus word was given as a starting point, and in one half of the experiments external distraction was caused.

These tests brought to light interesting results.   The sequence of words and sentences immediately recalled the speech as well as the writing of dementia præcox.   A definite direction of speech was excluded by the arrangement of the experiment. The stimulus word at most acted for some time as a more or less indefinite " theme."   Superficial connecting elements became strik- ingly manifest, corresponding to the disintegration of logical con- nections.   There were numerous perseverations, or repetitions of the preceding word, almost corresponding to the repetition of the stimulus words in our experiments, and besides this there were numerous contaminations,[62] and closely connected with them neologisms or newly formed words.

From Stransky's voluminous material I should like to quote

[61] Comp. Diagnost. Associationsstudien, I Beitrag.   B. Durchschnitts- berechnungen, Abschnitt III.

[62] Comp. Rud. Meringer and Karl Mayer: Versprechen und Verlesen. Eine psychologisch-linguistische Studie.   Stuttgart, Göschen, 1895.

By contamination we understand the condensation of many sentences or words into one sentence or into one word; e. g., " I will soon him see home " is a contamination of " I will go home," " I will soon see him."

a few examples by way of illustrations: " On one leg stand the storks, they have wives, they have children, they are those who bring the children, the children, which they bring into the house, this house, an idea, which people have about storks, about the activity of storks, the storks are large birds—with a long beak and live on frogs, frogs, freegs, frogs, the frogs are froogs, in the morning (Früh), in the morning they are with—breakfast (Frühstück), coffee, and with coffee they also drink cognac, and cognac they also drink wine, and with wine they drink everything possible, the frogs are large animals, and which the frogs devour, the storks devour the birds, the birds devour the animals, the animals are big, the animals are small, the animals are human beings, the animals are no human beings . . .", etc.

" These sheep are . . . were merino sheep, from which the fat was cut out by the pound, with Shylock was the fat cut out, the pound cut out," . . . etc.

" K . . . was a K . . . with a long nose, with a ramnose, with a rampnose, with a nose to ram, a ram gift, a man, who has rammed, who is rammed," etc.

From these examples of Stransky's experiments it can be readily seen what laws of association the stream of thought follows. It is mainly those of similarity, coexistence, motor speech connections and combinations of sound. Besides this one is struck by the numerous perseverances and repetitions (Sommer stereotypies). If we compare to this the sample of dementia præcox associations which we have just quoted from Miss Pelletier we find a striking similarity.[63] Here, just as there, one finds the same laws of similarity, contiguity, and assonance. Only stereotypies and perseverations are lacking in Pelletier's analysis,[64] although they can be plainly seen in the communicated material. Stransky also adds to these conspicuous similarities numerous nice examples taken from dementia præcox.

It is especially important that in Stransky's normal tests there

[63] We must, however, mention that the speeches of Stransky show the unmistakable character of precipitation which is generally lacking in dementia præcox. What gives the impression of precipitation is hard to say.

[64] As mentioned above, Sommer has already shown the sound associations and stereotypies in simple word reactions.

appear numerous word and sentence-conglomerations which can be designated as contaminations.[65]

Example: " Especially a meat, which one cannot get rid of, the thoughts which one cannot get rid of, especially when one ought to persevere at it, persevere, persevere, severere, severin," etc.

According to Stransky this conglomeration contains the following condensed series of ideas

(*a*) Mutton is consumed in England,

(*b*) This idea I cannot get rid of,

(*c*) This is perseveration,

(*d*) I am to talk at random whatever comes into my mind.

The contamination is therefore a condensation of various series of ideas.   It is essentially to be considered as a mediate association.[66]   This character of contamination can be clearly proven from Stransky's pathological examples:

Question: What is a mammal?

Answer (Pat) : It is a cow, for example a midwife.   Midwife is a mediate association of cow and shows the probable way of thought.   Cow—bears living young—human beings likewise—midwife.[67]

Question: " What do you understand by the Holy Virgin? '

Answer: " The behavior of a young lady."

As Stransky rightly observes the thought probably goes as follows: Immaculate conception—virgo intacta—irreproachable conduct.

Question: " What is a square?"

Answer: " An angular quadrate."

[65] By contamination we understand the condensation of many sentences or words into one sentence or into one word; e. g., " I will soon him see home " is a contamination of " I will go home."   " I will soon see him."

[66] See the analysis of mediate associations.   Diagnost. Associations-studien, Beitrage I, Introduction.

[67] According to Professor Blueler, the following combination is more probable:

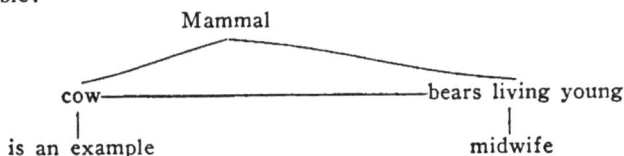

```
                    Mammal

     _____/_____
    /                                           \
  cow———————————————————————————bears living young
   |                                       |
is an example                           midwife
```

The condensation consists of:
(a) Square is a quadrate,
(b) The square has four angles.

From these examples it should be evident that the numerous contaminations appearing in distracted attention are somewhat similar to the mediate associations which appear under distraction in the simple word reactions. It is well known that our experiments have shown that in distractibility there is moderate increase of the mediate associations.

The concurrence of three experimenters, Stransky, myself, and dementia præcox, can be no accident. It proves the correctness of our conceptions and is another confirmation of the symptom of apperceptive weakness, which of all the degenerative symptoms of dementia præcox stands out most prominently.

Stransky points out that contamination has frequently produced such bizarre word formations that they unfailingly recall the neologisms of dementia præcox. That a great number of neologisms are really brought about in this manner I am convinced. Pointing to the picture of a horse a patient remarks,[68] " This is a domestic-burden," by which he means:
(a) The horse is a domestic animal,
(b) The horse is a beast of burden.

Based on clinical observation Neisser[69] remarked in 1898 that the newly formed words, which according to the rule as well as the roots are neither verbs nor nouns, are really no words at all but represent sentences inasmuch as they always serve to allegorize (Versinnbildlichung) a whole process. This expression of Neisser indicates the idea of condensation. He even goes so far as to talk directly about the allegorization of a whole process. Right here I should like to call attention to the fact that in his work " Die Traumdeutung "[70] Freud showed that there is a great

[68] Given by translators as play of words, in author's example can not be translated.
[69] Neisser: Über die Sprachneubildungen Geisteskranker. Vortrag. 74. Sitzung. d. Vereins Ostdeutsch. Irrenärzte in Breslau. Allgem. Zeitschr. f. Psych., LV, p. 443.
[70] Based on a large empirical material, Kraepelin, in his work, Über Sprachstörungen im Traume (Psychol. Arbeiten, Bd. V, H. I), also occupies himself with these questions. In reference to the psychological genesis of the phenomena in question, Kraepelin's assertions show that he

deal of condensation in dreams.   Unfortunately I am unable to discuss *in extenso* the extent and extremely valuable psychologic material of this as yet hardly recognized investigator.   It would lead too far.

A knowledge of this valuable book is presupposed.   No real refutation of the ideas of Freud have to my knowledge been advanced.   I confine myself to the affirmation that dreams having already many analogies to disturbance of the associations of dementia præcox, possesses also the special speech condensations in the sense of contaminations of whole sentences and situations.   Kraepelin too was struck by the resemblance between the speech of dreams and of dementia præcox.[71]   From the numerous examples which I observed in my own and other's dreams, I will mention only a very simple one, illustrating at the same time condensation and neologism.   One in his dream wishes to express approval of a certain situation and says: "That is fimous."

does not differ much from the views developed here.   Thus he says on p. 10: "The appearance of speech disturbances in dreams is certainly very closely dependent upon the obnubilation of consciousness and the diminution in clearness of ideas conditioned by it."

What Paul Meringer, Mayer and others designate as contamination, and Freud as condensation, Kraepelin names "ellipse" ("mixture of different series of ideas," "en elliptical concentration of several simultaneous series of thoughts").   Here I wish to call attention to the fact that as early as in the 80's Forel used the expression "ellipsis" for the condensations and new word formations in paranoid states.   It escaped Kraepelin that Freud had already, in 1900, treated dream-condensations in a detailed manner.

By condensation Freud designates the blending together of situations, pictures, and elements of speech.   The linguistic expression "contamination" concerns only the blendings of speech, and is, therefore, a special idea which is subordinate to Freud's idea of condensation.   The retention of the term contamination is to be recommended for condensation of speech.

[71] Arch. f. Psych., XXVI, p. 595.   Compare also Psych. Arbeiten, Bd, V, H. I, p. 79, where Kraepelin says: "It should perhaps be kept in mind that the peculiar expressions of the patients (dementia præcox) are not simple 'nonsense,' nor still less do they represent intentional productions of overbearing moods, but they are the expression of a peculiar disturbance of word findings which must be nearly related to those found in dreams."   Kraepelin also expresses the view that "in confusion of speech, besides disturbances of word selecting and the speech expression of thought, there are even such disturbances of the process of thought which in part resemble those of dreams."

It is a contamination of (a) fine, (b) famous.

The dream is likewise an apperceptive weakness par excellence, which is especially shown by its tendency towards symbolism.[72]

Finally there is still one more question which really should have been answered first, and that is: Does the state of consciousness in Stransky's normal experiments really correspond to one of disturbed attention? Before all it is to be noted that Stransky's experiments in distractibility show no essential changes from the experiments with the normal, consequently neither the association nor the attention in both conditions could have been so very different. But what is one to think of the disturbance in the experiments with the normal?

It seems to me that the main reason is to be looked for in the forced character of the experiment. The test persons were instructed to talk at random, and that they have at times talked with great rapidity is shown by the fact that on an average they uttered from 100 to 250 words per minute, whereas in normal speech the average per minute is only from 130 to 140.[73] Now if one talks and perhaps thinks more rapidly about indifferent things than he is accustomed to, he cannot bestow sufficient attention on the associations. A second point which has to be considered is the fact that most of the test persons were unaccustomed to the situation and it consequently influenced the emotional state. This may be compared to excited orators who develop a state of " emotional stupidity."[74] In such conditions I found extraordinarily high numbers of perseverations and repetitions. Emotional stupidity causes likewise great disturbance of attention. We can therefore take it as certain that in Stransky's experiments with the normal the attention was really disturbed, although the state of consciousness is surely not clear.

We are grateful to Heilbronner for an important observation.[75] By examining a series of associations in a case of hebe-

[72] Compare above the excellent observation of Pelletier, *l. c.*. Über das Symbol.

[73] Stransky: *l. c.*, p. 14.

[74] Jung: Über Simulation von Geistesstörung. Journ. f. Psych. und Neur., II, p. 191, und Wehrlin in Diagnost. Associationsstudien, Beitrag II.

[75] Monatsschr. f. Psych. und Neur., Bd. XVIII, Erg. Heft, p. 324.

phrenia he found that on one occasion forty-one per cent., on another twenty-three per cent. of the reaction words referred to the patients' environment. Heilbronner considers this circumstance as an evidence for the fact that the perseverations are derived from the " vacuum," *i. e.,* they are due to a deficiency of new ideas. I can confirm this observation from my own experience. Theoretically it would be interesting to know in what relationship this manifestation stands to the Sommer-Leupoldt symptom of " Benennen und Abtasten " (name and touch).

New and independent views on the psychology of dementia præcox are brought forth by Otto Gross.[76] He proposes the expression dementia sejunctiva for the name of the disease. The reason for this name is the disintegration of consciousness in dementia præcox, hence the sejunction of consciousness. The idea of sejunction Gross naturally takes from Wernicke. He could just as well have taken the older synonymous idea of dissociation (Binet, Janet). Fundamentally, dissociation of consciousness means the same thing as Gross's disintegration of consciousness. By accepting the idea of sejunction we have only a new term of which psychiatry has certainly enough. Dissociation according to the French school is a weakness of consciousness due to the splitting off of one or a series of ideas. They separate themselves from the hierarchy of the conscious ego and begin a more or less independent existence.[77] The hysteria doctrine of Breuer and Freud was developed on this foundation. According to the more recent formulations of Janet, dissociation is the result of " *abaissement du niveau mental* " which destroys the hierarchy and either favors or effects the origin of automatisms.[78] What automatisms are freed is most beautifully shown by Breuer and Freud.[79] The application made by Gross of this doctrine to dementia præcox is new and important. The funda-

[76] Gross: Über Bewusstseinszerfall.   Monatschr. f. Psych. und Neurol. p. 45.—Idem: Beitrag zur Pathologie des Negativismus. Psych.-neur. Wochenschr., 1903, Nr. 26.—Idem: Zur Nomenklatur " Dementia sejunctiva." Neurol. Centr.-Bl., 1906, Nr. 26.—Idem: Zur Differentialdiagnostik negativistischer Phänomene. Psych.-neurol. Wochenschrift, 1906, Nr. 37, und 38.
[77] See the fundamental work of Janet: L'automatisme psychologique.
[78] Janet: Les Obsessions.
[79] Studien über Hysterie.

mental idea of the author is expressed as follows: "Disintegration of consciousness in my sense signifies the simultaneous flow of functionally separated series of associations.   To me the chief point lies in the conception that the activity of consciousness is to be considered as a resultant of many synchronous psychophysical processes.[80]

These citations ought to illustrate sufficiently the author's ideas.   We can perhaps agree with the view that consciousness, or better, the content of consciousness, is the result of numerous nonconscious or unconscious psychophysical processes.   In contradistinction to the current psychology of consciousness, in which beyond the epiphenomenon "consciousness" there immediately begins the nutritive processes of the brain cells, this aspect is really a refreshing progress for psychiatry.   Gross seems to think that the psychic content (not the content of consciousness!) flows synchronously in single series of associations. This comparison seems to me somewhat equivocal.   I think it more correct to assume successive conscious-becoming ideational-complexes which are constellated by antecedent association-complexes.   The cement of these complexes is some definite affect.[81]   If the connection between Gross's synchronous series is severed by disease, disintegration of consciousness results. Translated into the language of the French school, it means that if one or more association series are split off there results a dissociation causing weakness of consciousness.   Let us not quarrel over words.   Here, too, Gross returns to the problem of apperceptive disturbance; he, however, approaches this problem from a new and interesting side, from the side of the unconscious. Gross attempts to uncover the roots of the numerous automatic phenomena which break into the consciousness of dementia præcox with elemental power and strangeness.   The symptoms of automatic phenomena in the conscious life of dementia præcox should be known to all psychiatrists.   They are the autochthonous ideas, the sudden impulses, hallucinations, the manifesta-

[80] Gross: Zur Nomenklatur, etc.

[81] The pure laws of association play quite an insignificant rôle when confronted with the unlimited power of the emotional constellation, just as in real life where the logic of thought has no significance when confronted with the logic of feeling.

tions of thought-influence, imperative ideas with the character of strangeness, the cessation and disappearance of thought (appropriately designated by one of my patients as " Gedankenentzug "— thought deprivation), and inspirations (pathological fancies), etc. Gross states that the catatonic manifestations are " changes of the will brought about by an agent which is conceived as external to the ego-continuity, and is therefore referred to as a strange power." They are a "substitution of the will of thef ego-continuity by a crowding in from outside of another conscious series." We have to keep in mind that many association series í can simultaneously flow in the organ of consciousness without influencing one another. From these series in consciousness one will have to become the carrier of the continuity of consciousness, while the other association series are then naturally " subconscious," or rather, " unconscious." Now at all times there is a possibility that also in these the nervous energy swells up and reaches such a stage that one of its end organs becomes endowed with attention, which means that a joint from the unconscious association series pushes itself illegitimately into the continuity of the dominant óne. If these conditions are fulfilled, the accompanying subjective process can be only of such a nature as any psychic manifestation entering into consciousness in an unadjusted manner, and is therefore perceived by the conscious continuity as something entirely foreign. Ideas of explanation are almost inevitably added, the referred psychic manifestation (idea) originating not from the ego-consciousness, but thrown into it from without.[82] As aforesaid, the displeasing part in this hypothesis is the assumption of synchronous independent association series. Normal psychology does not furnish us with any facts on this point. Where we can best observe split-off series of ideas, namely, in hysteria, we find that the opposite holds true. Even where one deals with apparently totally separated series, one can find somewhere in some hidden location the bridge leading from one series to the other.[83] In the mind all stands in connection with all, the present psyche is the result of milliards of constellations.

[82] Gross: Zur Differentialdiagnostik, etc., l. c.
[83] Just this point I have thoroughly proved (depending on Flournoy) in a case of somnambulism. Zur psychologic und pathologie sog. okkulter Phänomene. Leipzig, 1902.

Aside from this slight inconvenience, I believe that I may call Gross's hypothesis a rather happy one. It tells us in brief that the roots of old automatic phenomena lie in the unconscious association connections. If consciousness becomes disintegrated (*abaissement du niveau mental*—apperceptive weakness) the complexes accompanying it are freed from all restraint and are then able to break into the ego-consciousness. This is an eminent psychological conception, and agrees in the clearest possible manner with the doctrines of the French school, with the experience of hypnotism, and with the analysis of hysteria. If we weaken the power of consciousness by suggestion and produce thereby a split-off series of presentations, as, for example, in post-hypnotic commands, we find that this series reappears with a power inexplicable to the ego-consciousness. In the psychology of ecstatic somnambulists we have the typical breaking in of split-off ideas.[84]

Unfortunately Gross leaves one question open, and that is, which are the dissociated series of ideas and what is the nature of their content? Some time ago, long before Gross wrote, Freud answered this question very brilliantly. As far back as 1893 Freud[85] showed preliminarily that a hallucinatory delirium originates from an unfulfilled wish, and that this delirium is a compensation for unsatisfied yearnings, that the person takes refuge, as it were, in the psychosis in order to find in the dream-like delirium of the disease that which was refused to him in reality. In 1896 Freud analyzed a paranoid condition, Kraepelin's paranoid form of dementia præcox, and showed how the symptoms were accurately determined according to the scheme of the transformation mechanism of hysteria. Freud then stated that paranoia, or the group of cases belonging to paranoia, are a defensive neuropsychosis; that is to say, that just like hysteria and obsessions, they, too, originate from the repression of painful memories, and that the form of the symptoms is determined by the content of the repression.[86]

[84] See especially the magnificent script examples of Helene Smith, Flournoy: Des Indes, etc.

[85] Über den psychischen Mechanismus hysterischer Phänomene. Neurol. Centr.-Bl., 1893, H. 1 and 2.

[86] For further remarks on Defensive Neuropsychoses, see Neurol. Centr.-Bl., 1896.

In view of the far-reaching significance of such an hypothesis it pays to enter somewhat more fully into the classical analysis of Freud.

It was the case of a thirty-year old woman who manifested the following symptoms: She imagined that her environment had changed, she was no longer respected, she was annoyed, she was watched, and her thoughts were known. Later she thought that she was watched in the evening while undressing. She also experienced sensations in her abdomen which she believed were occasioned by an unseemly thought on the part of the servant girl. Visions then appeared in which she saw female and male genitals. Whenever she was with women alone she had hallucinations of female genitals, and at the same time imagined that the others saw her own genitals.

Freud analyzed this case. He observed that this patient behaved just like a hysteric; that is, she showed the same resistances, etc. What seemed unusual was the fact that the repressed thoughts did not appear, as in hysteria, in the form of loosely connected fancies, but in the form of hallucinations, and hence the patient compared them to her own voice. (I shall later take the opportunity to produce experimental proof for this observation.) The hallucinations here mentioned began to manifest themselves after the patient saw in the asylum a number of naked female patients bathing together. " It may be presupposed that the reason these impressions repeated themselves was because something of great interest was connected with them." She stated that she felt ashamed in the presence of these women. This somewhat forced and altruistic modesty was striking, and pointed to something repressed. Patient reproduced " a series of scenes from her seventeenth to her eighth year, during which, while bathing before her mother, her sister and her physician, she was ashamed of her nakedness. This series, however, reached back to a scene in her sixth year, when she undressed in the children's room before going to sleep without feeling ashamed of her brother, who was present. Finally it was found that for years the brothers and sisters were in the habit of showing themselves naked to one another before retiring." At that time she was not ashamed. " She is now trying to make up in shame what she lost as a child."

" The beginning of her depression began at the time of a disagreement between her husband and her brother, on account of which the latter no more visited her. She was always much attached to this brother."

Besides this she spoke about a moment in the history of her disease during which, for the first time, " everything became clear "; that is, during which she became convinced that her assumption about being generally despised and intentionally annoyed was true. She gained this assurance during a visit of her sister-in-law who, in the course of conversation, gave utterance to the following words: " If such a thing should happen to me I would not mind it." Mrs. P. at first took this lightly, but when her visitor left her it seemed to her that these words contained a reproach, meaning that she was in the habit of taking serious matters lightly, and since that hour she was sure that she was a victim of common slander. The tone in which her sister-in-law spoke was especially convincing. It was, however, shown that the sister-in-law spoke about another subject before giving utterance to this sentence. She related to the patient that in the father's home there were all sorts of difficulties with the brothers, and added: " In every family many things happen which one would rather keep in darkness, and that if such a thing should happen to her she would take it lightly. Mrs. P. had to acknowledge that her depression was connected with the sentences uttered before the last one. As she repressed both sentences which could recall her relations with her brother and retained only the last meaningless one, she was forced to connect with it the sensation of being reproached by her sister-in-law; but, inasmuch as the contents of this sentence offered absolutely no basis for such assumption, she disregarded it and laid stress on the tone with which the words were pronounced."

After this explanation Freud turned his attention to the analysis of the voices. " It is to be noted that such indifferent remarks as ' here goes Mrs. P.'—' she now looks for apartments ' were very painfully felt." The first time she heard voices was after she read the story " Heiterethei," by O. Ludwig. After reading it she took a walk on the highway, and suddenly while passing a peasant's cottage voices told her: " That is just how the house of Heiterethei looked! Here is the well and here the bush!

How happy she was in all her poverty!" The voices repeated whole paragraphs of what she had just read, but the contents were of an indifferent nature. The analysis showed that while reading she at the same time entertained extraneous thoughts and that she was excited by totally different passages of the book. Against this material analogy between the couple in the romance and herself and her husband, the reminiscences of intimate things of her married life and family secrets, against all these, there arose a repressive resistance because they were connected with her sexual shyness by very simple and demonstrable streams of thought, and finally resulted in the awakening of old experiences of childhood. In consequence of the censorship exercised by the repression the harmless and idyllic passages connected with the objectionable ones by contrast and vicinity became reënforced in consciousness, enabling them to become audible. For example, the first repressed thought referred to the slander to which the secluded heroine was subjected by her neighbors. She readily found in this an analogy to herself. She, too, lived in a small place, had no intercourse with anybody and considered herself despised by her neighbors. The suspicion against the neighbors was founded on the fact that in the beginning of her married life she was obliged to content herself with a small apartment. The wall of the bedroom, near which stood the nuptial bed of the young couple, adjoined the neighbors room. With the beginning of her marriage there awakened in her a great sexual shyness. This was apparently due to an unconscious awakening of some reminiscences of childhood of having played husband and wife. She was very careful that the neighbors should not hear through the adjacent wall either words or noises, and this shyness changed into suspicion against the neighbors." On further analysis of the voices Freud often observed "a character of diplomatic uncertainty. The morbid allusions were generally deeply hidden. The continuity of some sentences was marked by strange expressions, unusual forms of speech, and, in other ways, characteristics common to the auditory hallucinations of paranoiacs. The hallucinations also showed a slight disfigurement caused by compromise formation."

I have purposely given the floor to the author of the first analysis of paranoia, a thing so highly important for psychopathology.

I did not know how to abridge the ingenious demonstrations of Freud.

Let us now return to the question of dissociated series of ideas. We now see what meaning Freud gives to Gross's assumed dissociations. They are nothing other than the repressed complexes found in hysteria,[87] and last but not least also in the normal,[88] The mystery of repressed series of ideas reveals itself as a psychological mechanism of general significance and of quite usual occurrence. Freud puts in a new light the problem of incongruity between the content of consciousness and emotional tone discussed by Stransky. He shows that indifferent, even insignificant ideas may be accompanied by intense feeling tones which they take from a repressed idea. Freud uncovers a way which can lead us to the understanding of the inadequate feeling tone in dementia præcox. I need hardly discuss the significance of this. The results of Freud's investigations may be summed up as follows:

Both in form and in content of the symptoms of paranoid dementia præcox there are thoughts which in consequence of their disagreeable tone became unbearable to the conscious ego, and hence are repressed. They determine the nature of the delusions and hallucinations as well as the whole general behavior. Whenever apperceptive paralysis appears in a person the manifested automatisms contain the dissociated idea complexes—the whole army of subjected thoughts become unyoked. Thus we may generalize the result of Freud's analysis.

As everybody knows, Tiling,[89] uninfluenced by Freud, and based on clinical experience, came to conclusions closely resembling those of Freud. He, too, would contribute to individuality an almost boundless significance for the origin and formation of the psychosis. The importance of individual psychology is undoubtedly underestimated in modern psychiatry, owing less perhaps to theoretical reasons than to the helplessness of practical psychology. One can therefore cover a great distance with

[87] Compare Diagnost. Associationsstudien, Beitrag V, VI, VII, VIII.

[88] Diagnost. Associationsstudien, Beitrag IV.

[89] Tiling: Individuelle Geistesartung und Geistesstörung.—Idem: Zur Aetiologie der Geistesstörungen. Centr.-Bl. f. Nervenheilkunde u. Psych., 1903, p. 561.

Tiling, at any rate, even further than Neisser[90] thought he could go. At the question of etiology, that is, at the nucleus of the problem, one must halt. The individual psychology of neither Freud nor Tiling explains the origin of the existing psychosis. In the citation from Freud's analysis we very clearly see that the "hysterical" mechanisms uncovered by him suffice to explain the origin of hysteria, why then does a dementia præcox originate? We can readily understand why the content of the delusions and hallucinations are of such a nature and of no other; but why non-hysterical delusions and hallucinations should at all appear we do not know. Here at the basis of all there should be one physical cause embracing all the psychological ones. Let us assume with Freud that every paranoid form of dementia præcox runs according to the mechanism of hysteria, but why is the paranoid unusually stable and resistive, while hysteria is characterized by the great mobility of its symptoms? Here we strike against a new phase of the disease. As Neisser[91] puts it, the mobility of the hysterical symptoms is based on the mobility of the affects, while the paranoid state is characterized by the fixation of the affects. This thought extraordinarily important for dementia præcox is formulated by Neisser as follows:[92]

"From without only a very poor assimilation takes place. The patient is able to exert less and less voluntary influence on the stream of his ideas and in this manner there originate separate groups of idea complexes of much greater volume than in the normal. These complexes are, as to contents, connected by certain inherent personal relations, but hardly coalesce in any other way, so that depending on the momentary constellations it is now this and now that one which more intensively determines the direction of the continued psychic elaboration and association. In this way there results a disintegration of the personality which becomes so to say a passive spectator of the inflowing impressions from the various irritative sources and an inanimate puppet for the freed irritations thus generated. The affects normally

[90] Neisser, Individualität und Psychose.   Berlin, 1906.
[91] Neisser, Individualität und Psychose, p. 29.
[92] To be sure Neisser only does that for paranoia, under which he can hardly include original paranoia (Kraepelin). His representations fit mainly the paranoids.

destined to regulate our relations to our environments and to
direct our adaptation to the same, which are a protection to the
organism and represent the motive powers of self-preservation,
are alienated from their natural destiny.   Owing to the organ-
ically strong feeling tone of the delusional stream of thought, no
matter what the emotional state may be, this and this only is
always reproduced.   These fixations of the affects destroy the
ability of feeling joy or compassion and lead to an emotional
isolation of the patient which runs parallel with the intellectual
alienation."

Neisser describes here the familiar picture of apperceptive
dementia.   Lack of new acquisition, paralysis of purposeful progress (adapted to reality), disintegration of personality and
autonomy of complexes.   Finally, he adds the " Fixierung der
Affecte " (fixation of affects), that is, the fixation of the emotionally accentuated complexes (for affects have always regularly an intellectual content, though it is not always known).
From this he explains the emotional dementia (Masselon invented
for this the fitting expression " clotting ").   Following Freud,
fixation of affects means that the repressed complexes (the car-
riers of affects) can no more be disconnected from the contents
of consciousness, they remain and so prevent the further development of personality.

To avoid misconceptions I must here add that the continued
persistence of a strong complex in normal psychic life can lead
only to hysteria.   Yet the consequent manifestations of the hysterogenic affect are different from the symptom-complex of
dementia præcox.   For the origin of dementia præcox we must
demand a totally different disposition than we do for hysteria.
If a purely hypothetical supposition be permitted one could perhaps venture the following train of thought: The resultant manifestations of the hysterogenic complex are reparable, while the
affect of dementia præcox gives opportunity for the appearance
of an anomalous metabolism (toxine?), which injures the brain
in a more or less irreparable manner, so that in consequence of
this defect the highest psychic functions become paralyzed.   It
is for this reason that the acquisition of new complexes becomes
difficult or ceases altogether.   The pathogenic or rather the incit-
ing complex remains to the last, and the further development of

personality is definitely checked. In spite of an apparently gap-less causal chain of psychological events leading from the normal into the pathological, one can never disregard the possibility that in certain cases a change of metabolism (in the sense of Kraepelin) may be primary, whereby the accidental newest and last complex " clots " or " curdles," and thus inherently determines the symptoms. Our experience does not as yet reach far enough to warrant the exclusion of this possibility.

SUMMARY OF THE FIRST CHAPTER.

This anthology from the literature, in my judgment, shows quite distinctly that all the views and investigations which among themselves hardly exhibit any apparent connection nevertheless converge to the same point. The observations and intimations plucked from the different realms of dementia præcox point above all to the idea of a real central disturbance which is designated by different names, such as apperceptive dementia (Weygandt), dissociation, *abaissement du niveau mental* (Janet, Masselon), disintegration of consciousness (Gross), disintegration of personality (Neisser *et al.*). Then there arose the idea of tendency towards fixation (Masselon, Neisser) and from this Neisser adduces the emotional dementia. Freud and Gross find the important fact of the presence of split-off series of ideas. To Freud, however, belongs the credit of being the first to show in a case of paranoid dementia præcox the " principle of conversion " (repression and indirect reappearance of the complexes). Nevertheless the mechanisms of Freud do not reach so far as to explain why there originates a dementia præcox and not a hysteria ; hence it must be postulated that for dementia præcox there is a specific resultant manifestation of affects (toxins?) which causes the definite fixation of the complex by injuring the sum total of the psychic functions. However, the possibility cannot be disputed that the " intoxication " may appear primarily from " somatic " causes and seize the accidentally remaining complex and change it pathologically.

CHAPTER II.

THE EMOTIONAL COMPLEX AND ITS GENERAL ACTION ON THE PSYCHE.

My theoretical propositions for an understanding of the psychology of dementia præcox are in reality almost entirely exhansted in the contents of the first chapter, for Freud in his works on hysteria, imperative neuroses and dreams has, after all, given all essentials. Nevertheless our ideas gained on an experimental basis differ somewhat from those of Freud. Perhaps my conception of the emotional complex even oversteps the limits of Freud's views.

The essential basis of our personality is affectivity.[1] Thought and action are only, as it were, symptoms of affectivity.[2] The elements of our psychic life, sensations, ideas and emotions are given to consciousness in the form of certain entities, which can in a manner be compared to a molecule, if one may venture upon an analogy with chemistry.

To illustrate: I meet on the street an old comrade and imme-

[1] For feeling, mood, affect, and emotion, Bleuler proposes the expression "affectivity," which not only designates the affects in the proper sense but also the light feelings or feeling tones of pleasure and pain in every possible occurrence. Affektivität, Suggestibilität, Paranoia. Halle: Marhold. 1906. p. 6.

[2] Bleuler says (*l. c.*, p. 17): "In all our actions and omissions affectivity is a much greater motive element than reflection. It is likely that we act only under the influence of pleasure and pain, and it is chiefly due to the affects connected with them that logical reflections obtain their force. Affectivity is the broader conception of which volition and effort represent but one side."

André Godfernaux says: "The affective state is the dominating force, the ideas are nothing but its subjects. The logic of reasoning is only the apparent cause for the wheeling about of thought. Below the cold and rational laws of association of ideas there are others which conform more to the deep necessities of existence. It is the logic of sentiment." Le sentiment et la pensée et leurs principaux aspects physiologiques. Paris, Alcan, 1894.

diately an image is formed in my brain, it is a functional entity, the picture of my comrade X. We differentiate in this entity ("molecule") three components ("radicals"); sensory perceptions, intellectual components (ideas, memory pictures, judgments, etc.) and emotional tone.[3] These three components are firmly united, so that if the memory picture alone of X comes to the surface the elements appertaining to it are regularly always with it. The sensory perception is represented by an accompanying centrifugal stimulation of the sensory spheres concerned. I am therefore justified in speaking here of a functional entity.

Through some thoughtless gossip of comrade X, I once became involved in a very unpleasant affair, the consequences of which I suffered for a long time. This affair embraces a large number of associations (it can be compared to a body made up of a number of molecules), many persons, things and events are contained therewith. The functional entity "my comrade" is only one figure among many. The entire mass of memory has a definite feeling tone, a vivid feeling of anger. Every molecule participates in this feeling tone, so that as a rule it is always accompanied by this feeling, whether appearing alone or in connection with others, and the more identified it becomes with this great union the greater is the feeling tone.[4]

I once witnessed the following incident: I was taking a walk with a very sensitive and hysterical gentleman. The village bells were pealing a new and very harmonious chime. My companion,

[3] Compare Bleuler, *l. c.*, p. 5. "Just as we are able to distinguish in every sensation of light, even in the very simplest one, between quality, intensity, and saturation, so we may speak of processes of cognition, of feeling, of will, though we are well aware that no psychic process exists to which all three qualities are not common, even if it is now one, now the other that is in the foreground."

Bleuler therefore divides the "psychic forms" into preponderantly intellectual, preponderantly effective, and preponderantly voluntary.

[4] This can be directly compared to Wagnerian music. The *leitmotif* designates (in a measure like the feeling tone) an important complex presentation of the dramatic construction (such as Walhalla, Vertrag, etc.). Whenever an action or speech incites this or that complex, the *leitmotif* appertaining to it immediately resounds in some variation. It is exactly the same in ordinary psychological life. The *leitmotif* is the emotional tone of our complexes; our actions and moods are nothing but variations of our *leitmotif*.

who generally displayed great feeling for such tunes, suddenly began to rail at it, saying that he could not bear the disgusting ringing in the major key, that it sounded abominably, that this was an especially disagreeable church and unsightly village (the village is famous for its charming location). This remarkable and inadequate affect interested me and I continued my investigation. My companion then began to abuse the local parson. His reason for the abuse was that the minister had an ugly beard and—wrote very bad poetry. My companion, too, was talented lyrically. The affect then lay in poetic rivalry.

This example shows how the molecule (the chiming, etc.) takes part in the feeling tone of the whole mass of presentations[5] of the poetic rivalry. We designate this by the name of the emotionally accentuated complex. Considered in this sense the complex is a higher psychic entity. When we come to examine our psychic material, for example, that supplied by the association experiments, we find that every association belongs, as it were, to some complex. (I refer to Contribution IV ff. of the Diag. Assoz.-Stud.) To be sure, it is somewhat difficult to prove this in practice, but the more carefully we analyze the more we find that single associations belong to some complex. Undoubtedly they are related to the ego-complex more than any other. The ego-complex in the normal person is the highest psychic instance. By it we understand the ideational mass of the ego which we believe to be accompanied by the potent and ever-living feeling-tone of our own body.

The feeling-tone is an affective state which is accompanied by bodily innervations. The ego is the psychological expression for the firmly associated union of all general bodily sensations. The personality proper is therefore the firmest and strongest complex, and asserts itself (provided it be healthy) throughout all psychological storms. It is for that reason that the ideas which directly concern one's own personality are the most stable and interesting; in other words, they possess the strongest attention-tone. (Attention in the sense of Bleuler is a state of affectivity.[6])

[5] The individual presentations are connected among themselves according to the different laws of associations (similarity, coexistence, etc.). But the higher connections are grouped and selected by an affect.

[6] Bleuler: Affektivität, etc., p. 31, says: "Attention is nothing more than a special form of affectivity" (p. 30). "The attention just like all our

ACUTE EFFECTS OF THE COMPLEX.

Reality sees to it that the quiet circles of egocentric ideation are frequently disturbed by strong feeling tones, so called affects. A situation threatening danger pushes aside the tranquil play of ideas and places in its stead a complex of other ideas of the strongest feeling-tone. The new complex then appears very prominently, crowding all the others into the background. It totally inhibits all other ideas, retaining only those direct egocentric ideas which fit its situation. Under certain conditions it can even momentarily suppress to complete unconsciousness the strongest contrary ideas. It has the strongest attention-tone. (We therefore do not say we concentrate attention on anything, but the state of attention enters into this presentation. See " Diagnost. Assoc.-Stud.," I. Beitrag, Abschnitt B. L.)

Where does an ideational complex get its inhibiting or promoting force?

We have seen that the ego-complex on account of its union with the general sensations of the body is the most stable and richest in associations. The perception of a situation threatening danger excites fear. Fear is an affect, hence it is accompanied by physical conditions, by a complicated harmony of muscular tension and excitation of the sympathetic. The perception has therefore found the way to bodily innervation and in this manner has immediately helped its association-complex to get the upper hand. Owing to this fear numberless general sensibilities of the body become changed, changing thereby most of the sensations lying at the foundation of the general ego. Corresponding to this the ordinary ego loses its attention-tone (or its clearness, or its promoting and inhibiting influence on other associations or other synonyms). It is compelled to give way to the stronger and other general sensations of the new complex. Notwithstanding this, it does not normally perish but remains as a feeble affect-ego[7] because even very strong affects

actions is always directed by an affect," or better expressed, "Attention is a side of affectivity which does nothing but that which is already known of it, that is, it smooths the way for certain associations and inhibits others."

[7] The modification of the ego-complex resulting from the setting in of a markedly accentuated complex I designate as the " affect ego."

are unable to change all sensations lying at the foundation of the ego. As every-day experience shows, the affect-ego is a feeble complex, and is considerably inferior to the affect-complex in constellated force.

Let us now assume that the dangerous situation clears rapidly. The complex then soon loses some of its attention-tone, because the general sensations gradually resume their normal characteristics. Yet the affect continues to oscillate for a long time in its physical and hence also in its psychical components. "The knees shake," the heart continues to palpitate excitedly for some time, the face is either flushed or pale, "one can hardly recover from fear." From time to time, at first after short, and later after longer intervals, this picture of fear returns and is charged with new associations, thus exciting waves of affect-reminiscences. This perseveration of the affect, in addition to the great emotional force, also contributes towards the proportional increase in the number of the associations. Therefore extensive complexes are always of great feeling tone, and inversely, strong affects always leave behind extensive complexes. This is simply due to the fact that on the one hand strong complexes contain numerous bodily innervations, and on the other hand, strong affects can constellate many associations, owing to their strong and persistent excitement of the body. Affects may normally continue to act for a long time (in the form of disturbances of the stomach, heart, sleeplessness, trembling, etc.). Gradually, however, they die away, the complexes disappear from consciousness, and only occasionally in dreams there appear more or less hidden intimations. In the associations they continue to show themselves for years in characteristic complex disturbances. But their gradual extinction is prevented by a general psychological peculiarity, namely, their readiness to reappear in almost full force on similar or much weaker stimuli. For a long time after, there exists a condition which I should like to designate as complex-sensitiveness. A child once bitten by a dog will scream with

This modification will, as a rule in painful affects, consist of restriction and recession of many parts of the normal ego. Many other wishes, interests, and affects have to give way to the new complex, insofar as they oppose it. The ego in the affect is reduced to its lowest, as can be seen in such scenes as theater fires and shipwrecks, where in a trice all culture disappears, being replaced by the cruelest lack of consideration.

fear if it observes a dog even at a distance. People who have received a painful message will thereafter open all their mail with apprehension, etc. These complex effects, which under certain conditions will extend over long periods, leads us to the consideration of the

CHRONIC EFFECTS OF THE COMPLEX.

There are two kinds to be differentiated:

1. There is a complex-action which extends over a very long period and which is often evoked by a single affect.

2. There are special chronic effects which become lasting because the affect is always in a continuous state of provocation.

The first group is best illustrated by the legend of Raymundus Lullus, who, as a gallant adventurer, was for a long time enthusiastically courting a lady. Finally the longed for billet arrived inviting him for a nocturnal rendezvous. Lullus, full of expectation, arrived at the appointed place and as he approached the lady who was there awaiting him she suddenly parted her apparel and uncovered her bosom eaten away with cancer. This event made such an impression on Lullus that henceforth he devoted his life to pious asceticism.

There are impressions which last a lifetime. Indeed the lasting effects of strong religious impressions or shocking incidents are well known. The effects in youth are particularly strong. Education, to be sure, is based on this; that is, to impart lasting complexes to the child. The durability of the complex is guaranteed by a constantly active feeling-tone. If the feeling-tone becomes extinguished the complex, too, becomes extinguished. The persistent existence of a complex with feeling-tone has naturally the same constellating effect on the other psychical activities as an acute affect. Whatever suits the complex is taken up, everything else is excluded or at least inhibited. The best examples can be found in religious convictions. There is no argument, no matter how threadbare, that is not advanced if it is *pro,* on the other hand the strongest and most plausible arguments *contra* do not thrive; they simply glide by, because emotional inhibitions are more powerful than all logic. Even among people of intelligence who have great education and experience at their command, one sometimes observes a real blindness, a true systematic anæsthesia when an attempt is made to convince them of the doctrine of determinism. How often we notice that an old unpleasant impression will, in many people, produce an imperturbable false judgment that no logic, no matter how clear, can dislodge!

The effects of the complex extend not only over thought but also over action, forcing it continually in a very definite direction. How many people thoughtlessly practice religious rites and many other possible baseless actions, though intellectually they long since are above it all!

The second group of chronic complex-effects in which the feeling-tone is constantly sustained by actual stimuli, offer the best examples of complex constellations. The strongest and most persistent effects are especially seen in the sexual complexes where the feeling-tone is constantly maintained by unsatisfied sexual desire. A glance through the "History of the Saints," or, e. g., Zola's "Lourdes," or "Rêve," will show numerous examples. Nevertheless the constellations are not always of a totally coarse and sensuous nature, often they are finer influences, marked by symbolisms acting on thought and action. I refer to the numerous and instructive examples offered by Freud. Freud presents the conception of "symptom-action" as a special act of the constellation. (One should really speak of "symptom-thought" and "symptom-action.") In his "Psychopathologie des Alltagslebens" Freud shows that apparently fortuitous disturbances of our actions, such as lapses in talking and reading, forgetting, etc., are due to the infringement of constellated complexes. In his "Traumdeutung" he points out a similar influence in our dreams. In our experimental work we have proven that complexes disturb association experiments in a characteristic and regular manner. (Peculiar forms of reactions, perseveration, retardation or loss of reaction, subsequent forgetting of critical or post-critical reactions,[8] etc.) These observations give us val-

[8] Compare Jung: Experimentelle Beobachtungen über das Erinnerungsvermögen. Zentr.-Bl. f. Nervenheilk. u. Psychiatrie, 1905. Freud, too, says the following (Traumdeutung, 1900, p. 301): "If the report of a dream appears to me at first difficult to understand, I request the dreamer to repeat it. This he rarely does with the same words. The passages wherein the expressions are changed I recognise as the weak points of the dream's disguise. The narrator is admonished by my request that I mean to take special pains to solve the dream and immediately under the

uable indices for the complex-theory. In selecting my stimulus words I took care to employ as far as possible words in colloquial use, principally to avoid difficulties of understanding by the subject. It would be expected that an educated subject would react easily, but indeed this is not the case. At the very simplest words there appear obstructions and other disturbances which can be explained only by the fact that the stimulus word has excited a complex. But why should it be difficult to reproduce easily an idea which is closely connected to a complex? The emotional inhibition must be cited as the main hindering cause. The complexes exist mostly in a state of repression. As a rule one deals with most intimate secrets which are anxiously guarded and which one either does not wish to expose or is unable to do so. The repression may even under normal conditions be so strong that there exists a hysterical amnesia for the complex; that is, there is a feeling of an emerging idea, of a significant connection, but the reproduction is held back by vague hesitation. There is a feeling as though one wished to say something which immediately slipped away. That which slipped away is the complex-thought. Occasionally there appears a reaction which unconsciously contains the complex thought but the test person is blind to it, and it is only the experimenter who can lead him on in the right way. The repressing resistance may also show afterward a striking effect in the reproduction test. Amnesia influences by preference the critical and post-critical reactions. These facts show that the complex has a certain exceptional position in relation to the more indifferent psychic material. Indifferent reactions follow " smoothly " and generally have very short reaction times. They are always at hand for the ego-complex to dispose of at pleasure. It is different with the complex reactions! They appear only with opposition, and often when about to appear they again withdraw from the ego-complex. They are peculiarly formed; often they are the products of embarrassment, of which the ego-complex itself is unaware, often they merge into amnesia in contradistinction to the indifferent reactions which frequently possess great stability and are reproducible even after months and years. We see, then,

impulse of resistance protects the weak points of the dream's disguise, by replacing the treacherous expressions by remoter ones."

that the complex-associations are much less at the disposal of the ego-complex than the indifferent ones. From this it must be concluded that the complex takes a relatively independent position to the ego-complex, it is like a vassal who does not bow implicitly to the domination of the ego-complex. Experience also teaches that the stronger the feeling-tone of a complex, the stronger and more frequent will be the disturbances of the experiment. A person dominated by a complex of strong feeling is less able to react " smoothly," not only to association experiments but to all stimuli of daily life, for the uncontrollable influences of the complexes constantly exert hindrances and disturbances. His self-control (the control of his frame of mind, thought, words and actions) suffers in proportion to the strength of the complex. The purposefulness of his actions is more and more replaced by unintentional lapses, errors, and unaccountabilities for which he himself often can give no reason. A person with a strong complex shows, therefore, intensive disturbances during association experiments, for a great number of apparently innocent word stimuli excite the complex. The following two examples elucidate the aforesaid:

CASE I.   The stimulus word " white " has numerous intimate connections. The subject, however, could only hesitatingly react with " black." By way of explanation I obtained another series of reactions to " white." " The snow is white, so is the sheet covering the face of a dead person." The subject had recently lost a beloved relative. The intimate contrast " black " shows symbolically perhaps the same thing, that is, mourning.

CASE 2.   " Paint " excites hesitatingly the reaction " landscapes." This peculiar reaction is explained by the following successive fancies. " One can paint landscapes, portraits and faces—as well as cheeks if one has wrinkles." The subject, an old maid who sorrows over the departure of an admirer, bestows a loving attention on her body (symbolic action), thinking that by painting she will become more attractive. She adds, " One paints the face when one takes part in a theatrical performance. I took part once." It is to be noted that she took part in a theatrical performance when she was still in possession of her lover.

The associations of persons with strong complexes swarm with

such examples. But the association experiment is only one side
of the daily psychological life. The complex-sensitiveness can
also be shown in all other psychic reactions.

CASE 1. A young lady cannot bear to see the dust beaten out
of her mantle. This peculiar reaction is based on the fact that
she is somewhat masochistic. As a child her father frequently
chastised her by spanking her *a posteriori,* which eventually
caused sexual excitement. For this reason, to whatever even
remotely resembles this form of chastisement, she is forced to
react with marked rage, which rapidly changes into sexual excitement and masturbation. On saying to her once on a quite indifferent occasion, " You must obey," she went into a condition of
strong sexual excitement.

CASE 2. Mr. Y. falls in love with a lady who soon afterwards
marries Mr. X. In spite of the fact that Mr. Y. knew Mr. X.
for a long time and even had business transactions with him, he
again and again forgot his name, so that on a number of occasions, when wishing to correspond with X., he was obliged to ask
other people for his name.

CASE 3. A young hysterical woman was suddenly assaulted
by her lover during which she was especially frightened by the
erected member of the seducer. She was after the incident
afflicted with a stiff arm.

CASE 4. A young lady while frankly relating a dream, without
any apparent reason suddenly hid her face under a curtain. This
striking reaction of shame was explained by the analysis of the
dream which revealed a sexual wish.[9]

CASE 5. Many persons commit peculiar complicated acts
which at the basis mean nothing but complex-symbols. I know
a young lady who when promenading wished to take along a baby
carriage. The reason for this, as she blushingly admitted, was
because she desired to be looked upon as married. Elderly
unmarried women are wont to use dogs and cats as complex-
symbols.

As the aforesaid examples show, thought and action, both in
general and particular, are constantly disturbed and peculiarly
distorted by a strong complex. The ego-complex is, so to say,

[9] For further examples of symbolic actions see Beitrag. VI ff. of the
Diagnost. Assoz.-Stud.

no longer the whole personality, as alongside of it there exists another being, living in its own way and therefore inhibiting and disturbing the development and progress of the ego-complex, for the symptom-actions very frequently take up time and exertion which are thus lost to the ego-complex. We can readily imagine how the psyche is influenced when the complex increases in intensity. The most lucid examples are always furnished by the sexual complexes. Let us take as an instance the classical state of being in love. The lover is possessed by his complex. All his interests hang only on this complex and the things belonging to it. Every word, every object recalls to him his sweetheart (experimentally even apparently indifferent word stimuli excite the complex). The most insignificant objects are guarded like priceless jewels, corresponding to their value in the complex. The whole environment is considered *sub specie amoris.* Whatever does not suit the complex glides by; all other interests sink to nothing, hence there results a standstill and a temporary reduction of the personality. Only that which suits the complex excites affects and is psychically elaborated. All thought and action move in the direction of the complex. Whatever is not impressed into this direction, is repudiated, or is accomplished with superficiality, unemotionally, and without any care. In attending to indifferent affairs there will appear the most peculiar compromise-productions; in business letters, lapses referring to the love-complex slip in, and in conversation one finds suspicious mistakes. The flow of objective thought is constantly interrupted by the incursions of the complex. Many pauses of thought result which are filled in by episodes of the complex. This well-known paradigm shows clearly the influence of a strong complex on the normal psyche. We see how all psychic energy is entirely bestowed on the complex at the expense of all the other psychic material which in consequence remains unused. All the other stimuli which do not suit the complex undergo a partial apperceptive dementia and emotional reduction. Even emotional tone becomes inadequate. Insignificant things, like little ribbons, dried flowers, pictures, *billets-doux,* hair, etc., are treated with the greatest care, while vital questions are often treated laughingly or indifferently. On the other hand the slightest remark touching the complex even remotely, immediately excites violent anger and painful outbreaks which may assume disproportionate dimensions. (In a case of dementia præcox we may note that when asked whether he is married, the patient falls into inadequate laughter or he begins to cry and becomes completely negativistic, or he shows an obstruction, etc.) Had we not the means to look into the mind of a normal lover we would have to consider his behavior that of a hysteric or catatonic. In hysteria where the complex-sensitiveness reaches a higher grade than in the normal, we lack almost all means of penetrating the mind and are obliged to laboriously habituate ourselves to enter into the feelings of hysterical affects. We totally forego this in catatonia, perhaps because we do not as yet know enough about hysteria.

The psychological state of being in love can be designated as a possession-complex. Besides this special form of sexual complex which for didactic reasons I have chosen as a paradigm for the complex of possession (it is the most common and best known form), there are naturally many other kinds of sexual complexes which can similarly exert a strong influence. Among women one frequently finds complexes of unreciprocated or even hopeless love. In such cases one generally notes an extremely strong complex-sensitiveness. The slightest intimations on the part of the other sex are assimilated into the complex and elaborated with a total blindness for the weightiest arguments against them. An insignificant utterance of the adored one is construed as a powerful subjective proof. The accidental interests of the one desired become similar interests to the adoring woman—a symptom-action which often rapidly vanishes if the wedding finally takes place or if the object of adoration is changed. The complex-sensitiveness manifests itself also in an unusual sensitiveness to sexual stimuli, which especially appears in the form of prudery. Those possessed of the complex at an early age ostentatiously avoid everything that may call up sexuality—the familiar " innocence " of grown-up daughters. They know indeed everything, where it lies and what it signifies, but there whole behavior is as if they never had the slightest notion of things sexual. If· the subject must be broached for medical purposes one at first believes that he is on virgin soil, but he soon finds that all the necessary knowledge implicitly exists, only the patient does not

know where she got it from.[10]   A psychoanalysis usually finds
that behind numerous resistances there is hidden a complete rep-
ertoire of fine observations and subtle deductions.   In a somewhat more advanced age prudery often becomes unbearable, or
there appears a naïve symptomatic interest for all kinds of
society news in which "one ought to take an interest because
one is of an age when . . ., etc." The objects of those symptomatic interests are brides, pregnancies, births, scandals, etc.
The cleverness of elderly ladies for the last is proverbial.   These
interests pass then under the flag of the "objective, purely human,
interests." Here we simply have a transference; the complex
must under all circumstances assert itself.   As the sexual complex cannot in many cases assert itself in a normal manner,
it makes use of by-ways.   During the age of puberty they exist
in the form of more or less abnormal fancies, frequently alter-
nating with religious ecstatic phases (transferences).   In men,
sexuality (if not directly lived through) is frequently changed to
a feverish professional activity or to some eccentricity, such as
dangerous sports, etc., or to peculiar academic passions, such as
a collecting mania.   Women take up some altruistic activity
which is usually determined by the special form of the complex.
(They devote themselves to nursing in hospitals where there are
young assistant physicians, etc.)   Or there may be strange eccen-
tricities, affectations, "putting on airs" which shall express distinction and proud resignation.   The artistic predispositions are
especially wont to gain by such transferences.[11]   One very frequent manner of transference is hiding the complex by means
of a contrasting frame of mind.   This manifestation is frequently
seen in those who are constantly endeavoring to banish a chron-
ically irritating sorrow.   Among these one generally finds the
best wags, the finest humorists whose jokes however are spiced
with a grain of bitterness.   Others hide their pain under a forced
and convulsive cheerfulness, which, on account of its boisterous-
ness and artificiality (lack of emotion) allows of no ease in
society.   Women betray themselves by an unbridled aggressive

[10] Freud expresses himself in a similar manner. Compare also the case
in Beitrag VIII, Diagnost. Assoz.-Stud.

[11] Freud calls this transference "sublimation": Drei Abhandlungen zur
Sexualtheorie. Deuticke, Leipzig und Wien, 1905, p. 76.

gayety, the men by sudden disproportionate alcoholic and other excesses (also fugues!). These transferences and simulations may, as is known, produce real double personalities, which have long excited the interest of writers with a psychological trend (see Goethe's " Zwei-Seelen-Problem," and among the modern writers Herman Bahr, Gorki, *et al.*). "Double personality" is not a mere literary term, it is a fact in natural science of general interest to psychology and psychiatry, especially when it manifests itself in the form of double consciousness or dissociation of personality. The dissociated complexes are always differentiated by peculiarities of mood and character, as I have shown in a case of the kind.[12]

It happens not seldom that the transference gradually becomes stable and at least superficially replaces the original character. Every one knows people who when judged by their exterior are considered very gay and entertaining. Inwardly, or under circumstances seen in private life, they are sullen grumblers nurturing an open wound. Frequently the true nature suddenly breaks through the artificial investment, the assumed blithesomeness suddenly disappears and we are then confronted with a new person. A single word, a gesture, striking this wound, shows the complex lurking within the soul. Such imponderabilities of human emotional life must be borne in mind when we enter with our coarse experimental methods into the complicated mind of the diseased. In association experiments with patients who suffer from marked complex-sensitiveness (as in hysteria and dementia præcox) we find exaggeration of these normal mechanisms; hence their description and discussion will require more than a mere psychological *aperçu*.

[12] Jung: Zur Psychologie und Pathologie sogenannter okkulter Phänomene. Leipzig, 1902.
Comp. also Paulhan: La simulation dans le caractère.

CHAPTER III.

How the complex manifests itself in association experiments we have discussed a number of times, and the reader is therefore referred to our earlier publications. We must, however, return to one point which is of theoretical value. We frequently meet with complex reactions which are built up in the following manner:

1.	to kiss	—to love	3.0″
	burn	—ing	1.8″
2.	to despise	—someone	5.2″
	tooth	—teeth	2.4″
3.	friendly	—amiable	4.8″
	dish	—fish	1.6″

The first reaction of the three examples contains the complex (in 1 and 3 we deal with erotic references and in 2 with an injury). The second group of reactions shows a perseverating feeling-tone from the preceding reactions, as can be readily seen by their slightly prolonged reaction time and their superficiality. As explained in the first contribution of the " Diagnost. Assoz.-Stud.," associations like tooth—teeth belong to the motor-speech combinations, burn—ing to word completion and dish—fish to rhyme combinations. When attention is distracted, there is an increase in motor-speech combinations and in sound reactions, as was positively shown from the results obtained in distraction experiments. Whenever there is a diminution of attention there is an increase in the superficial associations and their value diminishes. Therefore, if during an association experiment without any artificial distraction there suddenly appear striking superficial associations, one is justified in supposing that a momentary diminution of attention has taken place. The cause of this is to be sought in an internal distraction. According to instructions the subject is supposed to fix his attention on the experiment, if his attention decreases, that is, if without any external reason the attention is turned away from the meaning of the stimulus word there must be an internal cause for this distractibility. We find this mostly in the antecedent or in the same reaction. There appears a strongly emotional idea, a complex, which on account of its strong feeling tone, assumes great distinction in consciousness, or when repressed sends an inhibition into consciousness, and in this way either suspends for a short time the effect of the directing idea (attention to the stimulus word) or simply diminishes it. The correctness of this supposition can usually be proven without any difficulty by analysis.[1] The phenomenon described is therefore of practical value as a complex-indicator. Of theoretical value is the fact that the complex need not be conscious for the subject. From the repression it can send an inhibition into consciousness, thus disturbing the attention; in other words, it can check the intellectual functioning of consciousness (prolongation of reaction time), or can make it impossible (errors), or can diminish its value (sound associations). The association experiments merely show us the details, whereas clinical and psychological observation show us the same phenomena in gross outlines. A strong complex, such as a tormenting grief, hinders concentration; we are unable to tear ourselves away from the grief and direct our activity and interests into other channels. When we make an attempt to do this, " to drown our sorrow," we succeed perhaps for a short time, but we are able to do it only " half-heartedly." Without our knowing it at the time, the complex prevents us from giving ourselves up entirely to our tasks. We undergo all possible inhibitions, during pauses of thought (deprivation of thought in dementia præcox) there appear fragments of complexes, which just as in association experiments, produce characteristic disturbances in intellectual functioning. We make mistakes in writing according to the rules of Meringer and Mayer,[2] we produce condensations, perseverations, anticipations, etc., and especially Freud's errors, which last reveal by their content the determining complex.

[1] For the technic of the analysis see Diagnost. Assoz.-Stud., VI and VIII Beitrag, and Jung: Die psychologische Diagnose des Tatbestandes. Jurist.-psych. Grenzfragen, 1906.

[2] Versprechen und Verlesen etc., Stuttgart, 1895.

Our lapses in talking are at critical points, that is, the words we say have a complex significance. We make mistakes in reading because we think that we see in the text words of the complex. Frequently the complex words appear in the peripheral field of vision[3] (Bleuler). In the midst of our diversions we are surprised to hear ourselves sing or whistle a certain melody, the text of which can only seldom and with effort be found, and is a complex constellation; or we continue to murmur a word, frequently a technical term, or any foreign word, which also refers to the complex. Sometimes we may be dominated by an obsession, a melody or word continually thrusting itself into our mind. Here, too, are complex constellations.[4] Or we may draw lines on paper or on the table, complex signs which are frequently not difficult to decipher. Wherever the complex disturbances refer to words we find displacements by sound-similarity or phraseological combinations. I refer here mainly to Freud's examples.[5]

I mention the following from my own observations: To the stimulus word " lawn " a gentleman reacts with the peculiar association " broker." The analysis readily shows that he was contemplating some transactions with a loan office—" pawn-broker."[6] The word-automatism, " Bunau-Varilla,"[7] by free associations gave the following series: " Varinas-Manila—Zigarillo—Havana cigar." It was because I forgot my matches that I resolved not to throw away the butt of my cigar, so as to light another good cigar with it. The word " Bunau-Varilla " appeared just at the moment when I was about to throw it away. A boy who won a prize for passing a brilliant examination in arithmetic continues to chant for hours the word " rithmication."[8]

[3] The greatest distinctness lies in the point of fixation where, too, is the greatest attention, hence for the peripheral field of vision attention is diminished, and the inhibition for the unsuitable is less than in the point of fixation, therefore in this location it is easier for repressed complex-fragments to manifest themselves.

[4] See examples in Beitrag IV Diagn. Assoz.-Stud. Compare also the mediate associations Beitrag I, Abschnitt B. III.

[5] Psychopathologie des Alltagslebens and Traumdeutung.

[6] Given by translators as play of words, in author's example can not be translated.

[7] Beitrag I, Diagnost. Assoz.-Stud.

[8] [Example given by translators. The example in the German text does not lend itself to translation. Ed.]

These examples serve to illustrate that which Freud treats conclusively in his " Traumdeutung," namely, that repressed thoughts
disguise themselves in similarities, be it in speech similarities
(sound), or similarities of optical pictures. For the latter forms
of displacement dreams afford the best examples.

Those who reject Freud's analysis of dreams can discover rich
substitutes in melody automatisms. At a merry entertainment
some one remarked that if a person marries he should marry a
proud lady. A gentleman present who recently married a woman
noted for her pride began to softly whistle to himself the melody
of a familiar street song. I immediately asked this gentleman
whom I knew well to tell me the text of this melody. I received
the following answer: " What I whistled just now? Oh that's
nothing, I believe I heard it often in the streets but I do not
know the words." I insisted that he should recall the words
which I knew well, but he was unable to do so; on the contrary
he assured me that he never heard these words. The text reads
as follows:

" Meine Mutter hat gesagt: Nimm dir keine Bauernmagd."
(" My mother has said do not take a peasant maid.")

During an excursion, a young lady accompanied by a gentleman whose proposal she soon hoped for quietly sang the Wedding March of Lohengrin.

A young colleague who just finished his doctor's thesis had to
whistle for half a day Handel's " Lo the conquering hero comes
crowned with glory," etc.

An acquaintance who was happy over a new and lucrative position betrayed himself by the following melody which obsessed
him: " Are we not born for glory? "

A colleague meeting a nurse during his rounds, who was supposed to be pregnant, immediately afterwards finds himself
whistling: " There were once two royal children who loved each
other so much."

I do not wish to increase unnecessarily this collection of melody
automatisms, every person can daily make the same observation.
We learn from this another method of disguise of the repressed
thought. It is well known that whistling or singing is a frequent
accompaniment in those occupations where the full attention is
not required (Freud), the rest of the attention can therefore

suffice to produce a dreamy movement of complex-thoughts. The conscious activity, however, prevents the complex from becoming clear, hence it can only show itself indistinctly, and this eventually happens in the melody automatisms which contain the thought of the complex in a general metamorphosed form. The resemblance lies in the situation or in the frame of mind; as, " Lo the conquering," etc., Bridal March, " There were once two royal children, etc.," or in the expression (" My mother has said, etc."). The complex-thought in these cases was not clear to consciousness, but manifested itself more or less symbolically. How far such symbolic constellations can go is best seen in the wonderful example of Freud in his " Psychopathologie des Alltagslebens." From the sentence *" Exoriar aliquis nostris ex ossibus ultor "* Freud was able to trace back to the forgotten word *" aliquis "* [a—liquis—liquid—fluid—blood miracle of S. Gennario—] the thought of a much overdue period in the beloved. I shall quote a similar example from my own experience in order to corroborate Freud's mechanisms.

A gentleman wishes to recite the familiar poem (" Ein Fichtenbaum steht einsam ") " A pine tree stands alone, etc." In the line " he felt drowsy " he becomes hopelessly stuck. With the words " with white sheet" he forgot everything. This forgetting in such well known verse seemed to me rather peculiar and I let him reproduce what came into his mind with the words " with white sheet." The following series resulted: " White sheet makes one think of the cloth for the dead—a linen cloth with which one covers a dead person—(pause)—now I think of a near friend—his brother died quite recently—he is supposed to have died of heart disease—he was also very corpulent—my friend is corpulent, too, and I thought it might also happen to him—probably he does not exercise enough—when I heard of this death I suddenly became frightened, it could also happen to me, as we in our family are predisposed to obesity—my grandfather also died of heart disease—I too find myself somewhat too corpulent and have therefore within the last few days begun treatment for reducing fat."

From this example it can be clearly seen how the repression draws out of consciousness symbolic similarities and chains them to the complex. This gentleman unconsciously identified himself with the pine tree which was enveloped in a white sheet.

From this fact it can also be assumed that he wished to recite this poem as a symbolic act in order to effect a discharge of his complex excitement. Another preferred realm of complex-constellation is the joke of the pun type. There are persons who possess special talent for this and among whom I know some who have very strong complexes to repress. What I mean I should like to show in a simple example which may serve as an illustration.

At a gathering there was a gentleman who made many good and bad puns. While oranges were being served he made the following pun: " O—rangierbahnhof " (shunting station). Mr. Z., who obstinately disputed the complex theory, called out: " You see, doctor, here you could again suppose that Mr. X. thinks about a journey." Mr. X. embarrassingly replied: " That is really the case; lately I thought much about travelling, but could not get away." Mr. X. thought particularly about a journey to Italy, hence the constellation through the oranges, a number of which he recently received from a friend in Italy. To be sure, at the moment of pronouncing the pun the meaning of it was totally unknown to him, for the complex constellation is, and must remain, obscure.

Dreams, too, are constructed according to the nature of the examples mentioned, that is, they are symbolic expressions of repressed complexes. In dreams we find very fine examples of symbolisms used for expression.[9] As is known, Freud finally advanced the dream investigations on a way towards progress. Let us hope that psychology will soon take cognizance of this fact. It would profit immensely by it. As for the conception of expression by means of symbolisms in the psychology of dementia præcox, Freud's " Traumdeutung " is epoch-making. In view of the importance of symbolic expression in dementia præcox it will not appear superfluous if I add another to the dream analyses reported in Contribution No. VIII of dream analyses. A friend[10] related to me the following dream:

" I saw how horses were hoisted by thick cables to indefinite heights. One of them, a powerful brown horse which was tied

[9] See examples in proof of this in Beitrag VIII, Diagnost, Assoz.-Stud.
[10] I am well acquainted with the personal and family relations of this gentleman.

up in a belt and dispatched upward like a package, especially took my fancy. Suddenly the cable broke and the horse dropped to the street. I thought that it was surely killed when, all at once, it started up and galloped away. At the same time I noticed that the horse was dragging along the heavy trunk of a tree, and I wondered how, in spite of that, it could advance so rapidly. Evidently it became skittish and was liable to do some damage. Then a rider on a small horse came along and slowly rode towards the unruly horse which also assumed a somewhat slower gait. Nevertheless, I feared that the horse might run over this rider when a cab came along and paced in front of the rider, thus bringing the horse to a still slower gait. I then thought now all is well, the danger is over."

I then took up the individual points of the dream and asked my friend X. to repeat to me whatever came into his mind at each point. The hoisting up of the horses recalled to him the idea of hoisting horses on a sky scraper and indeed they seemed to be covered up just like horses that are lowered into mines to work. X. recently saw in a periodical the picture of a sky scraper in process of building where the work is done at a dizzy height and at the same time thought that it was hard work that he would not care for. I then attempted to analyze this strange picture of hoisting a horse into the air. X. stated that the horse was tied around by a belt just as they used to tie horses which they lowered into the mines. What particularly struck the dreamer in the picture of the periodical was the work at such a dizzy height. The horse in the mines must also work. Perhaps the expression for mines (Berg-Werk, literally translated mountain-work) gave origin to the two thoughts of the dream, " mountain " expressing height and " work " expressing labor. I therefore asked X. to concentrate his mind on the word " mountain " and tell me the associations following it. He immediately remarked that he was a passionate mountain climber and especially about the time of the dream he had a great desire to make a high ascent and also to travel. But his wife felt very uneasy about it and would not allow him to go alone. She could not accompany him, as she was pregnant. For the same reasons they were obliged to give up a journey to America, whither they had planned to go together. They then realized that as soon as one has children it becomes more difficult to move about and one cannot go everywhere. (Both are very fond of travelling and formerly travelled much.) The idea of relinquishing his trip to America was especially unpleasant to him, as he carried on commercial transactions in that country and always hoped that perhaps by a personal visit to the country he would benefit commercially. On this hope he built many vague plans for the future, rather lofty and flattering to his ambition.

Let us briefly summarize that which has been so far said. Mountain can be interpreted as height. To ascend a mountain = to get to the top. Work = labor. The underlying sense of this may be " By labor one gets to the top." The height in the dream is especially plastically produced by the " dizzy heights " of the sky scrapers which designated America, where my friend's expectations lie. The picture of the horse which is evidently associated with the idea of labor seems to be a symbolic expression for " hard labor," for the work on a sky scraper upon which the horse was hoisted is very difficult, as is also the work which is accomplished by horses lowered into mines. In colloquial language we have such expressions as " work like a horse " and " harnessed like a horse."

By disclosing these associations we gain a certain insight into the sense of the first part of the dream. We have found the way which apparently leads us to very intimate hopes and expectations in the dreamer. Let us then assume that the sense of this part of the dream signifies, " By labor one gets to the top." The dream pictures appertaining to it can easily be taken as symbolic expressions for this thought.

The first sentences of the dream read: " I saw how horses were hoisted by means of thick cables to an indefinite height. One of them, a powerful brown horse which was tied up by a belt and dispatched upward like a package, especially took my fancy." This seems to contradict the analysis which is that by labor one gets to the top. To be sure one can also be hoisted up. In this connection X. recalls how he often looked with disgust upon those tourists who had themselves hoisted up to the high summits by the " flour sack " method. He never needed anybody's help. The various horses in the dream are therefore others who were unable to get to the top by their own effort. The expression

" like a package " seems also to express some contempt. But where in the dream is the dreamer himself represented? According to Freud he must be represented and indeed he is generally, the chief actor. He is undoubtedly the " powerful brown horse." A powerful brown horse resembles him firstly because it can work much, then the brown color is generally described as " a healthy reddish brown color " such as mountain climbers are wont to have. The brown horse then is probably the dreamer. It is hoisted up like the others—the content of the first two sentences seem to be exhausted to the last point. The hoisting up of the dreamer is not clear, it even contradicts directly the applied sense " through work one gets to the top."

It seemed to me of special importance to find out whether my supposition that the brown horse represents the dreamer was really confirmed. For this reason I asked him to concentrate his attention on the passage " I remarked that the horse dragged along a big trunk of a tree." He immediately recalled that formerly he was nicknamed " tree " on account of his powerful stout figure. My supposition was therefore correct, the horse had even his name attached. The trunk on account of its heaviness encumbered the horse, or at least should have done so, and X. wondered that in spite of that it advanced so rapidly. To advance is synonymous with to get to the top. Therefore in spite of the burden or encumbrance X. advances and indeed so rapidly that one gets the impression that the horse is skittish and may perhaps cause some misfortune. On being questioned X. stated that the horse could have been crushed by this heavy trunk if it had fallen, or the force of this moving mass could have thrust the horse into something.

These associations exhausted the fancies of this episode. I therefore began my analysis from another point, that is, at that part where the cable broke, etc. I was struck by the expression " street." X. stated that it was the same street in which his business was where he once hoped to make his fortune. One deals here with the hope for a definite career of the future. To be sure it came to nought, and if it would have come to anything it would have been due not so much to his position or his own merits as to personal influences. Hence we get the explanation for this sentence, " The cable broke and the horse dropped

down." It symbolically very properly expresses the disappointment. He did not fare like many others who get to the top
without any trouble. The others who were "preferred" to him
and got to the top could not begin to do anything of value for
"what could a horse do up there?" They were, therefore, in a
place where they could not do anything. The disappointment
over his failure, was, as he stated, so great that on one occasion
he was almost desparing of his future career. In his dream "he
thought" that the horse was "killed" but soon he verified with
satisfaction that it rose again and galloped away. He therefore
could not be subdued. Here apparently commences a new part
of the dream which probably corresponds to a different period
of his life, if the interpretation of the preceding part be correct.
I asked X. to fix his attention on the horse galloping away. He
states that for a moment in his dream he saw another but very
indistinct horse appearing near the brown one; this, too, dragged
the trunk and started to gallop away with the brown one, but it
soon became very indistinct and disappeared. As shown also by
the late reproduction, this horse seems to be under a special
repressing influence and hence important to the dream. X. therefore dragged the log with some one else and this person must
have been his wife with whom he is harnessed "in the yoke of
matrimony." Together they pull the trunk. In spite of the
burden which encumbers his progress he gallops away. This
again expresses the thought that he can not be subdued. The
galloping horse recalls to X. Welti's painting "Eine Mondnacht"
(a moonlight night) which represents galloping horses on a cornice among which one very distinct fiery horse is mounting. In
the same picture there is the representation of a married couple
lying in bed. The picture of the galloping horse (which at first
galloped with another) leads therefore to the very suggestive
painting of Welti. Here we get a very unexpected view into
the sexual nuance of the dream, whereas we thought we saw only
the complex of ambition and future career. The symbol of the
horse which until now showed only the side of the hardworking
domestic animal now assumes a sexual significance which is
specially confirmed by the horse scene on the cornice. There
the horse is the symbol of the passionate impulsive desire which
without any further discussion can be identified with the sexual

desire. As shown by the above-mentioned recollections, the dreamer feared that the horse would fall or that the force of the moving trunk might thrust it into something. This *vis a tergo* can readily be perceived as X.'s own impetuous temperament which he feared might sometimes force him into many thoughtless acts.

The dream continues: Then a rider on a small horse came along and slowly rode toward the unruly horse which also assumed a somewhat slower gait. His sexual impetuosity is bridled. X. states that the rider by his dress and from his general appearance resembled his superior. This fits the first interpretation of the dream. His superior moderates the rash pace of the horse; in other words, he hinders the too rapid advancement of the dreamer because he is his superior. Now we have to search for the further development of the sexual thought. Perhaps there is something behind this peculiar expression, "a little horse." X. states that the horse was little and pretty like a child's toy and recalls to him an incident of his youth. While still a boy he noticed a woman far advanced in pregnancy, wearing hoops. It was then the style. This appeared to him very comical and he asked his mother whether this woman wore a horse under her dress. (He thought of horses worn at carnivals or circuses which are buckled to the body.) Since then, whenever he saw a woman in a pregnant state, it recalled to him this childish hypothesis. His wife, as we mentioned above, is pregnant. Pregnancy was also mentioned above as a hindrance to travelling. Here it bridled the impetuosity which we were obliged to designate as sexual. This part of the dream apparently means that pregnancy of the wife imposes restraints on the husband. Here we have a very clear thought which is evidently intensely repressed and extraordinarily well hidden in the meshes of the dream. It is composed entirely of symbols of the upward striving conduct. Pregnancy, however, does not seem to be the only reason for the restraint, for the dreamer feared "that the horses may in spite of all overrun the rider." But then we have the slowly advancing cab which moderated still more the gait of the horse. On asking X. who was in the cab, he recalled that there were children. The children therefore were apparently subjected to some repression, as the dreamer recalled them only on being questioned. In the vulgar expression known to my friend it was "a whole car full of children." The wagon with the children inhibits his impetuosity. The sense of the dream is now perfectly clear. It reads as follows:

The pregnancy of the wife and the problem of too many children restrained the husband. This dream fulfills a wish as it presents the self-restraint as accomplished. At first sight the dream, just as all others, seems senseless, but when its first stratum is uncovered it already shows distinctly the aspirations and the disappointments of an upward struggling career. Inwardly, however, it hides a most personal question which must be accompanied by many painful feelings.

In the analysis and treatment of this dream, I omitted to refer to the numerous recurring analogous combinations, the similarity of pictures, and allegorical representations of phrases, etc. A careful examination of the reported observations shows that they contain the characteristic features of mythological thinking. I only wish to point out that the ambiguity of the individual pictures of the dream (Freud's overdetermination) simply shows the obscurity and haziness of thought in dreams. The pictures of the dream belong to one as well as the other complex of the waking state, although both complexes are sharply separated in the waking state. Due to a deficiency of the discriminating ability in the dream both complexes may at least symbolically flow together.

This manifestation is perhaps not clear without further explanation, but we can readily deduct it from our former premises.[11]

Our experiments in distraction confirm our supposition that in

[11] For the fusion of simultaneously existing complexes we may find some corroboration in the elementary fact not unknown in psychology (Féré in La pathologie des émotions, mentions it by way of intimation) that two stimuli simultaneously existing in two different sensory spheres, reinforce or respectively influence each other. From researches with which I am at present occupying myself, it seems to show that a voluntary motor activity is visibly influenced by a simultaneously existing automatic activity (breathing). From all that we know of complexes they are continued automatic incitements or activities. Just as they influence the conscious activity of thought so do also the complexes act upon one another formatively, so that every complex contains elements of the other, a thing which may psychologically be designated as fusion. Freud from a different point of view calls this Uberdeterminierung (overdetermination).

diminished attention, thought is rather superficially connected. The state of diminished attention expresses itself in a decrease of clearness of ideation. Whenever the ideas are not clear their differences, too, are not clear; hence our sensitiveness to differences is naturally diminished, for it is nothing but a function of attention or clearness (synonyms). Therefore there is nothing to prevent the mistaking of one idea (" psychic molecule ") for another, although normally they are clearly defined. The experimental expression for this fact is the increase of mediate associations produced by the distractibility. (See Beitrag IB of the " Diagnost. Assoz.-Stud.") It is known that the mediate associations of the association experiments (especially in a condition of distraction), are generally nothing else than a displacement of an intimate connection by phrase or sound. (For example, see Beitrag I. Intr. " Diagnost. Assoz.-Stud.") On account of the distraction the psyche becomes uncertain in the choice of expression, and has to be satisfied with all sorts of errors in the speech and acoustic systems, thus resembling a paraphasic.[12] We can readily assume the external distraction in our experiments to be replaced by a complex which displays its autonomous effect beside the activity of the ego-complex. We have discussed above the resulting association phenomena. Whenever the complex becomes excited the conscious association becomes disturbed and superficial, due to an escape of attention (or inhibition of

[12] Kraepelin (Uber Sprachstörungen im Traume, Psychol. Arbeiten, Bd. V, H. 1) is of the opinion that the proper formation of a thought is hindered by the encroachment of a distracting by-idea. On p. 48 he expresses himself as follows: " The common feature in all these observations (Dream paraphasias) is the displacement of the basal thought by the entrance of a by-association for an essential link of the chain of presentations. The derailment of speech or of thought to a by-association is due in my opinion, to lack of distinctness in the ideas." Kraepelin further asserts that " the by-idea causing the displacement of thought was distinctly a narrower and more significant idea which suppressed the more general and more shadowy one." Kraepelin calls this symbolic manner of derailment " metaphoric paralogia " in contradistinction to the purely " displacing " and " derailing paralogia." The " by-associations " are mostly perhaps associations of similarity—at all events we deal here very frequently with such—it is therefore easily understood how the paralogia has the character of metaphor. Such metaphors may give the impression, as it were, of an intentional disfigurement of the dream-thought. In this point Kraepelin is not very far from Freud's ideas.

attention) to the *a parte* existing complex. During the normal activity of the ego-complex the other complexes must be inhibited else the conscious function of the directed association would be impossible. We therefore see that the complex can only indirectly reveal itself by indefinite symptomatic association (symbolic actions), all of which show a more or less symbolic character.[13] (See all examples mentioned above.) The effects emanating from the complex must in the normal be weak and obscure because they are not in possession of their full attention which is taken up by the ego-complex. Therefore in the experiment on distraction the ego-complex and the autonomous complex must be directly compared to both psychic activities, just as in the experiment most of the attention is bestowed on the writing and only a fraction on the association, so in activity most of the attention lies in the ego-complex while the autonomous complex receives only a fraction of it (provided the autonomous complex is not abnormally excited). It is for this reason that the autonomous complex can think only superficially and vaguely, that is, symbolically. Its productions (automatism, constellations) which it sends into the activity of the ego-complex and into consciousness must be created in a similar manner.

We shall here give a brief analysis of the symbolic. We use the symbolic in contradistinction to the allegoric. Allegory is an intentional interpretation of a thought reinforced by emblems, while symbols are only indistinct by-associations of a thought, causing more vagueness than perspicuity. Says Pelletier:[14] " The symbol is a very inferior form of thought. One can define the symbol as a false perception of a relation of identity or of a very great analogy between two objects which in reality present but a

[13] Stadelmann (Geisteskrankh. u. Naturwissensch., München, 1905) in his regretably affected manner of representation, says: " The psychotic furnishes the partially or completely deranged feeling of his ego with a symbol, but unlike the normal he does not compare this feeling with other processes or objects, but it is stretched to such an extent that the picture which he has brought in for comparison he allows to become a reality, a subjective reality which in the judgment of others is a delusion." " The genius finds the necessity of forms in his inner life which he projects outwardly, and whereas the symbolized associations in the psychotic become delusions, in the genius it only manifests itself as a somewhat exaggerated experience."

[14] L'Association des Idées dans la Manie aigue, etc. Thèse de Paris, 1903.

vague analogy." Pelletier also presupposes that for the origin of symbolic association there must be a deficiency in power of discrimination. Let us now apply these reflections to the dream.

At the onset of sleep there is the suggestive imperative, "you wish to sleep, you don't wish to be disturbed by anything."[15] This is an absolute command for the ego-complex which subdues all associations. But the autonomous complexes as shown above are no more under the direct control of the ego-complex. They allow themselves to be pushed back quite far, and to be reduced, but not to be completely lulled to sleep. For they are like small secondary minds having their own affective roots in the body and by means of which they always remain awake. During sleep the complexes are perhaps just as inhibited as during the waking state, for the imperative call to sleep inhibits all side thoughts.[16] Nevertheless, just as during the noises of the day and in the waking state, so they succeed from time to time in presenting to the sleeping-ego their pale, apparently senseless, by-associations. The complex thoughts themselves are unable to appear, as the inhibition of sleep-suggestion is especially directed against them. If they are able to break through the suggestion, that is, if they can come to the full possession of attention, of course sleep immediately ceases. We see this very frequently in the hypnosis of hysterics; the patients sleep a short time, then they suddenly

---

[15] Of course this is only a figurative expression for the sleep obsession, or sleep instinct (see Claparède: Esquisse d'une théorie biologique du sommeil. Archives de Psychologie, Tome IV, p. 246). Theoretically I agree with the point of view formulated by Janet: *Par un côté le sommeil est un acte; il demande une certaine énergie pour être décidé au moment opportun et pour être accompli correctement.*" Les Obsessions, I, p. 408. Like every psychic process, sleep probably has its special cell chemism (Weygandt!). In what it consists no one knows. Considered from the psychological side it seems to be an autosuggestive phenomenon (Forel and others utter similar views). Thus we understand that there are many transitions from the pure suggestive sleep to the organic sleep obsession which gives the impression of a poisoning by some metabolic toxin.

[16] The instinctive sleep inhibition can be expressed psychologically as "*désintérêt pour la situation présent*" (Bergson, Claparède). The effect of the "*désintérêt*" on the association activity is the "*abaissement de la tension psychologique*" (Janet) which as afterwards described manifests itself in the characteristic association of dreams.

become awakened through fright from some thought-complex. Insomnia in many cases is due to uncontrollable complexes against which the energy of the auto-suggestion of sleep can no more be effective.   If, however, by proper means we reinforce the energy of such persons they are again able to sleep, because they can restrain their complexes.   But restraining the complex means nothing more than the withdrawal of the attention, that is, its distinctness.   Hence in their thought the complexes depend only on a small fraction of distinctness and because of deficiency of discrimination they manifest themselves in rather vague and symbolic expressions and become mingled.   A real censorship of dream-thoughts in the sense of Freud we need not admit.   The inhibition emanating from the sleep-suggestion perfectly suffices to explain all.   In conclusion we must mention another characteristic complex-effect, that is, the inclination to contrast-association.   As was fully shown by Bleuler (see Chap. I) psychic activity tending towards an aim must be accompanied by contrasts.   This is absolutely necessary for proper coördination and moderation.   From experience we know that every decision is accompanied by the association of contrasts.   Normally we are never impeded by contrasts, they only induce reflection and are useful for our actions.   But if for any reason the energy is impaired, then the individual readily becomes the victim of an opposition between positive and negative, inasmuch as the feeling-tone of the decision suffices no more to overpower and restrain the contrasts.   We see this very often wherever a strong complex absorbs the energy of the individual.   The energy being diminished, the attention for everything not belonging to the complex becomes superficial, and the associations lack a firm course.   As a result we get on the one hand shallow associations, and on the other the contrast can no longer be suppressed.   Sufficient examples can be found in hysteria where one deals entirely with contrasting emotions (see Bleuler's works) and in dementia præcox where we deal with emotional and speech contrasts (see Pelletier's work).   Stransky experimentally found speech contrasts in his forced talking.

A few general remarks will be made on the manner and course of the complex by way of addition to Chapters II and III.

Every emotional event becomes a complex.   If it does not meet an already existing kindred complex it is only of momentary significance, and gradually sinks with lulled emotional tone into the latent mass of memory where it remains until a kindred impression reproduces it. But if an emotional event meets an already existing complex, it reinforces it and for some time assists it in gaining the upper hand. The clearest examples of this kind are to be seen in hysteria, where apparently insignificant things may lead to strong emotional outbursts. In such cases the impression touched either directly or symbolically the rather loosely repressed complex and in this manner called forth a complex-storm, which, in view of the unimportance of the event, appears entirely disproportionate. The strongest complexes unite themselves with the strongest emotions and impulses. We must therefore not be surprised at the fact that most complexes are of an erotic-sexual nature (as are also most dreams and hysterias). Especially in women where the sexual is the center of psychic life there hardly exists a single complex not in relation to sexuality. The significance of sexual trauma for hysteria universally assumed by Freud probably rests on this circumstance. At any rate, sexuality should always be kept in mind during psychanalysis which does not, however, mean that all hysterias are exclusively traced to sexuality. Any strong complex may call forth hysterical symptoms in those predisposed, at least so it seems. I do not mention here all the other kind of complexes, as I have already attempted to sketch the most frequent kinds.[17]

It is for the interest of the normal individual to free himself from any obsessing complex which impedes the further proper development (adaptation to environment) of his personality. Time generally takes care of that. Frequently, however, artificial aid must be invoked so as to help the individual rid himself of an obsessing complex. Transference we have learned to know as a very frequent help. One is wont to grasp at something new, especially something which strongly contrasts with the complex (masturbatic mysticism). An hysteric can be cured if one is able to produce a new complex which will obsess her.[18]   Soko-

[17] Arch. für Krim.-Anthropol., 1906.

[18] Hysteria makes use of all sorts of detailed measures in order to protect itself against the complex, such as conversion into bodily symptoms, disassociations (splitting) of consciousness, etc.

lowski[19] expresses himself in a similar manner. If one succeeds in repressing the complex, there remains for a long time a strong complex-sensitiveness, that is, there is a marked tendency to recrudescence. If the repression was produced by compromise-formation there exists a lasting inferiority, a hysteria, in which only limited adaptation to the environment is possible. If the complex remains entirely unchanged which, to be sure, is possible only when there is most serious damage to the ego-complex and its functions, we must then speak of dementia præcox.[20] Of course, I speak here only from the psychological side and only affirm what one may find in the psyche of dementia præcox. The view expressed in the above sentence in no way excludes the idea that the inveterate persistence of the complex may be due to an internal poisoning which may perhaps have been originally liberated by the affect. This assumption seems probable because it is consonant with the fact that in most cases of dementia præcox the complex is in the foreground, while in all primary intoxications, such as alcoholic, uremic poisoning, etc., the complex plays a subordinate rôle only. Another fact which speaks for my supposition is that many cases of dementia præcox begin with striking hysteroid symptoms, and only during the course of the disease do they " degenerate," that is, only during the course of the disease do they merge into the characteristic stereotypy or senselessness. It was for this reason that the older psychiatrists spoke directly of degenerative hysterical psychoses. We may, therefore, formulate the above conceptions in the following manner:

Considered from without we see the objective signs of an affect. These signs gradually (or very rapidly) grow stronger and more distorted so that to ingenuous observation it finally becomes impossible to assume a normal psychic content and one then speaks of dementia præcox. A more perfect chemistry or anatomy of the future will perhaps sometime be able to demonstrate the objective metabolic changes belonging to it, or the toxin effects. Considered from within, which, of course, is only

[19] St. Petersburger Medic. Wochenschr., 1895.

[20] A similar? idea, which, however, is unfortunately almost choked by its weedy exuberant conception is uttered by Stadelmann, Geisteskrankh. u. Naturwissensch. München, 1905.

possible through complicated analogical conclusions, we observe that the subject can not psychologically free himself from a certain complex. Because he continually associates with this complex and allows all his actions to be constellated by it, there must result a certain reduction of personality. How far the purely psychological influence of the complex reaches in such case we are unable to say at present; we may, however, suppose that the toxin effect plays an important part in the progressive degeneration.

CHAPTER IV.

DEMENTIA PRÆCOX AND HYSTERIA.

A PARALLEL.

To write an exhaustive comparison between dementia præcox and hysteria would be possible only if we knew more thoroughly the disturbances of the association activities of both diseases, and especially the affective disturbances in normal individuals. At present we are far from this. What I intend to do here is to recall the psychological resemblances based on the preceding discussions. As a later treatment of the association experiments in dementia præcox will show, an antecedent comparison between dementia præcox and hysteria is necessary in order to understand the manifestations of the associations in dementia præcox.

I. THE DISTURBANCES OF THE EMOTIONS.

The more recent investigators of dementia præcox (Kraepelin, Stransky and others) group the emotional disturbances about the central point in the picture of the disease. On one side one speaks of emotional dementia, and on the other of an incongruity between ideation and affect (Stransky).

I do not speak here of terminal dementia as seen in the terminal stages of the disease which can hardly be compared to hysteria (they are two totally different diseases), but I limit myself to the apathetic conditions during the acute stages of the disorder. The emotional apathy so striking in many cases of dementia præcox has a certain analogy to the " *belle indifférence* " of many hysterics who describe their complaints with smiling serenity, thus giving a rather inadequate impression, or speak with equanimity about things which should really profoundly touch them. In Contributions VI and VIII of the " Diagnost. Assoz.-Stud." I endeavored to point out how the patients apparently speak unemotionally about things which to them are of the most intimate significance. This is especially striking in analyses where one occasionally discovers the reason for the inadequate behavior. So long as the complex connection which is under special inhibition does not become conscious, the patient may tranquilly speak about it in a rather light manner and without going into detail. This manner of light talking may result in a condition of evasion producing contrasting actions. I had a hysterical patient under observation who, whenever she was tormented by a depressing complex, entered upon an unbridled jovial behavior, thus repressing the complex. When she related anything very sad which really should have deeply moved her, she accompanied it by loud laughter. At other times she spoke with absolute indifference (the accent, however, betrayed her deliberateness) about her complexes as if they did not in the least concern her. The psychologic reason for this incongruity between the ideational content and the affect seems to be due to the fact that the complex is autonomous and allows itself to be reproduced only when it wishes. Hence we see that the *"belle indifférence"* of hysterics does not last very long but is suddenly interrupted sometimes by a wild emotional explosion, a crying spell, or something similar. We notice the same in the euphoric apathy of dementia præcox. Here, too, we see, from time to time, now an apparently unexpected moodiness, now a violent act, or a striking freak, which have nothing in common with the former indifference. Professor Bleuler and I have frequently noticed at our joint examinations that as soon as analysis succeeded in laying bare the complex, the apathetic or euphoric mask immediately disappeared and was replaced by an adequate affect often quite a stormy one, just as in hysteria when the sore spot is touched. There are, however, cases in which the obstructions defending the complex can in no way be penetrated. The patients then continually give contemptuous and meaningless answers, that is, they simply do not enter into the question, and the more direct bearing the questions have on the complex the less they answer.

Not seldom we see that after intentionally or unintentionally producing complex stimuli in apparently apathetic patients, there subsequently appears a reaction having a distinct relation to the stimulus. The stimulus therefore acted after a certain period of incubation. In my experience with hysterical cases I frequently observed that in conversation the patient spoke with an apparently affected indifference and superficiality about certain critical points so that this pseudo-self-control surprised me. But a few hours later I would be called to the ward because this very patient had fallen into a spell. It was then ascertained that the trend of the conversation subsequently attained an affect. The same thing can be seen in the origin of paranoid delusions (Bleuler). Janet[1] observed in his cases that at the time of the event which should have really acted as an excitant they remained calm, but after a latent period of a few hours or even days the corresponding affect manifested itself. I can confirm this observation of Janet. Baelz[2] observed on himself, during an earthquake, the manifestations which he calls " emotional paralysis."

The affective states without adequate ideational content which are so frequent in dementia præcox have likewise their analogies in hysteria. Let us for example recall the state of anxiety in obsessive neuroses! Here as a rule the ideation is so inadequate that even the patients recognize it by its logical instability and rate it as senseless, yet it seems to be the source of anxiety. That this is not so is shown by Freud, in a manner which until now has not been refuted and we can only confirm it. I recall the patient from Contribution VI of " Diagnost. Assoz.-Stud.," who had the obsession that she infected her minister and physician with her obsessive ideas. In spite of demonstrating to herself that this idea was totally unfounded and senseless, it did not cease to cause her intense anxiety. The frequent depressions in hysteria are in a great many cases referred by the patients to reasons which can only be predicated as concealing-reasons (Deckursachen). Really one deals with normal reflection and thought which is hidden in the repression. A young hysterical woman suffered from such a marked depression that at each answer she causelessly burst into tears. Her depression she obstinately and exclusively referred to a pain in her arm which she accidentally felt while at work. It was finally found that she had a love affair with a man who refused to marry her, which was the real cause of her constant vexation. Therefore before we state that the precocious dement is depressed for reasons

[1] If I identify here the cases described by Janet in his Obsessions with hysteria, it is because I cannot differentiate Janet's obsessed from hystericals.

[2] Allg. Ztschr. f. Psych., Bd. 58, p. 717.

inadequate we have to represent to ourselves the mechanisms existing in every normal person, which always tend to repress the unpleasant and to bury it as deeply as possible.

The explosive excitements in dementia præcox may be brought about in the same way as the explosive affects in hysteria. Every person treating hysteria is acquainted with the sudden affect and acute exacerbations of the symptoms. Frequently we are confronted with a psychological riddle and deem it sufficient to note " patient is again excited." But a careful analysis always discovers a clear reason for the excitement; now it is a careless remark from those about her, now a certain letter, or the anniversary of a critical event, etc. To liberate the complex, a mere nuance, perhaps only a symbol will suffice.[3] So also in dementia præcox, by careful analysis one may frequently find the psychological thread leading to the cause of the excitement. Of course we do not find this in all cases, the disease is too opaque for that, but we have absolutely no reason to suppose that no sufficient connections exist.

That the affects in dementia præcox are probably not extinguished but only peculiarly transposed and blocked, we see on rare occasions when we obtain a complete catamnestic view of the disease.[4] The apparently senseless affects and moodiness are subjectively explained by hallucinations and pathological fancies which can with difficulty or not at all be reproduced during the height of the disease because they belong to the complex. If a catatonic is constantly occupied by hallucinatory scenes which crowd themselves into his consciousness with elemental force and with a much stronger tone than the external reality, we can then without any further explanations readily understand that he is unable to adequately react to the questions of the physician.

[3] Thus Riklin mentions the following instructive example: A hysterical patient periodically vomited all milk she took. The analysis during hypnosis showed that while patient lived with a relative he once assaulted her sexually as she went to the stable to fetch some milk. "*Ibi homo puellam coagere conatus est, ut semen, quod masturbatione effluebat, ore reciperet.*" During the week after the hypnosis patient nearly always vomited what milk she took, though she had total amnesia for the hypnosis. Analytische Untersuchungen der Symptom und Assoziationen eines Falles von Hysterie. Psych.-Neurol. Wochenschr., 1905.

[4] See Forel: Autobiography of a case of acute mania, and Schreber: Denkwürdigkeiten eines Nervenkranken. Mutze, Leipzig.

Furthermore, if the patient, as described by Schreber, perceives other persons in his environment as fleeting shadows of men, we can again understand that he is unable to react adequately to the stimuli of reality, that is, he reacts adequately, but in his own way.

The lack of self-control or the inability to control the affects is characteristic of dementia præcox. We find this defect wherever there is a morbidly enhanced emotivity, especially in hysteria, epilepsy, etc. The symptom only shows that there exists a marked disturbance of the ego-synthesis, that is, there exist powerul autonomous complexes which no longer submit to the hierarchy of the ego-complex.

The lack of affective rapport so characteristic of dementia præcox we also frequently meet in hysteria, where we are unable to chain the personality and penetrate into the complex. In hysteria, to be sure, this is only temporary, because the intensity of the complex is rather fluctuating, but in dementia præcox, where the complex is stable, we can get an affective rapport only for the moment if we get the power to penetrate into the complex. In hysteria we gain something by this penetration, but in dementia præcox we gain nothing, for immediately thereafter we are again confronted by the personality of dementia præcox just as cold and strange as before. Under certain circumstances one may by means of analysis even cause a flaring up of the symptoms. In hysteria, on the contrary, a certain loosening takes place when the analysis is over. Whoever has penetrated into the mind of a hysteric by means of analysis knows that he has thereby gained a moral power over the patient (this is also true of confessions among normal individuals). But in dementia præcox, no matter how thorough the analysis may be, everything remains as before. The patients cannot enter into the mind of the physician, they adhere to their delusional assertions, they attribute hostile motives to the analysis, they are, and in a word, they remain uninfluenced.

2. CHARACTEROLOGICAL ABNORMALITIES.

The characterological disturbances claim an important position in the symptomatology of dementia præcox, though one can really not speak of "dementia præcox character." Yet one might just as well speak of it as of a "hysterical character" into which, as every one knows, all kinds of prejudices are smuggled, such as moral inferiority and many similar ones. Hysteria creates no character, but only exaggerates the already existing qualities. In hysteria we find all temperaments, we have the egotistic and altruistic personalities; criminals and saints, sexually excited and sexually frigid natures, etc. Indeed what really characterizes hysteria is the existence of powerful complexes which are incompatible with the ego-complex. Under the characteriological disturbances of dementia præcox we might mention the embellishment; that is, mannerism, affectation, mania for originality, etc. This symptom we frequently meet in hysteria and especially often whenever the patients think themselves out of their social element. This embellishment is especially frequently seen in the form of pretentious and studied behavior among women of a lower station coming in contact with those socially above them, such as dressmakers, maids, servants, etc.; also among men who are dissatisfied with their social standing and who are attempting to put on the appearance of those of a higher education and more imposing station. These complexes readily connect themselves with aristocratic gaits, with literary and philosophic enthusiasms and "original" views and expressions. They manifest themselves in exaggerated manners, and especially in studied speech, such as bombastic expressions, technical terms, affected eloquence and high-sounding phrases. We therefore find this peculiarity especially in such cases of dementia præcox as entertain any form whatsoever of the delusion of social elevation (Delir der Standeserhöhung of v. Krafft-Ebing).

In this case the disease takes over the mechanism from the normal, that is, from the caricature of the normal (hysteria), but the embellishment contains nothing specific in itself. Such cases show a special inclination to neologisms which are employed as learned or otherwise distinguished sounding technical terms. One of my patients named them "power-words" (Machtwörter) and showed a special liking for all possible peculiar expressions which to her seemed quite pregnant. The "power-words" serve to elevate and garnish the personality as much as possible. The expressive emphasis of the "power-words" accentuates the value of the personality against doubt and enmity, hence they are frequently used in dementia præcox as defensive and conjuring formulæ. A precocious dement under my care, whenever the doctors refused to grant him anything, threatened them with the following words: " I grand duke Mephisto will have you treated with blood revenge for Orang-Outang-representance." Others use the " power-words " to conjure the voice.[5] (See, *e. g.,* Schreber's " Denkwürdigkeiten.")

This embellishment is also expressed in gesture and writing; the latter, as is known, is especially decorated with all kinds of peculiar flourishes. We find a normal analogy to this, for example, in young girls who, out of capriciousness, imitate an especially marked or original script. Precocious dements frequently have a characteristic writing. The contrasting tendencies of their psyche are in a way expressed by their script, which is sometimes low and flowing, now precipitous, now large and now small. The same thing can readily be observed in temperamental hysterics, where one may demonstrate without any difficulty that the script variations begin at a complex. In the normal we also observe disturbances associated with complexes.

The tendency to embellishment is of course not the only source of neologisms. A great many originate from dreams and especially from hallucinations. Not seldom we meet with analyzable speech contaminations and sound-associations, the origin of which can be explained according to principles treated of in the preceding chapters. (For excellent examples see Schreber.) The origin of the " word-salad " can be explained by Janet's conception of the *" abaissement du niveau mental."* Many patients who are somewhat negativistic and refuse to consider the questions show " etymological " inclinations, inasmuch as instead of answering they disjoint the question and eventually furnish it with sound-associations. This is nothing else than a transference and concealment of the complex. They do not wish to consider the questions and direct themselves therefore to the sound manifestations. (For the analogy of not taking up the stimulus word see Contr. VIII Diagnost. Assoz.-Stud.) There are many indications besides to show that the sound features of speech are more striking to precocious dements than to other patients, since they so frequently occupy themselves with word-dissection

---

[5] Resembles the " Conjurations " of Janet (Les Obsessions).

and interpretations.[6]   The unconscious shows a special tendency towards new speech formation.   (See the " Himmelssprachen " of the classical somnambulists, and especially the interesting creations of Helene Smith.)[7]

Regardlessness, narrow-mindedness, and an inaccessibility to persuasion, we find both in the normal and pathological spheres, especially when accompanied by affective causes.   Under certain conditions there need only exist a firm religious or other conviction to make a person careless, cruel and narrow-minded.   There is no necessity to assume for this an emotional dementia.   On account of their excessive sensitiveness hysterics become egotistic and inconsiderate, and in this manner they torment themselves as well as their fellow beings.   For this, too, there need be no dementia, it is simply a blinding through the affect.   Indeed I must here again repeat the already often-mentioned restriction, namely, that between hysteria and dementia præcox there is only a resemblance of the psychological mechanism, but no identity.   In dementia præcox these mechanisms reach much deeper perhaps because they are complicated by toxic effects.

The silly behavior of the hebephrenic finds its analogy in the Moria states[8] of hysterics.   I had under observation for some time a hysterical woman of high intelligence who frequently suf-

[6] Forel's patient (Arch. f. Psych., XXXIV) was forced to make many such interpretations, thus, for example, she interpretated the name Vaterlaus as " *pater laus tibi.*" A patient of mine complained of the allusion which was made by means of the food. He had lately found in his food a linen thread (Leinenfaser). He guessed that it referred to Fräulein Feuerlein (an earlier acquaintance) with whom however he had certainly had no intimate relations. One of my patients complained one day to me that he could not understand what " a green figure " had to do with him. He got this idea because they put chloroform into his food. (chloros, forma).

[7] In examinations of unconscious writing (" Psychographie ") it can especially be well observed how the unconscious plays with the presentations. The words are not seldom written in a reversed sequence of letters or there are singular conglomerations of words in otherwise clear sentences. Under constellations of spiritualistic convictions attempts are made towards formation of a new language. The most prominent medium known is Helene Smith (comp. Flournoy, Des Indes à la Planète Mars). Similar manifestations I have reported in my work: Zur Psych. u. Path. sog. occulter Phänomene.

[8] Fürstner: Arch. f. Psych., Bd. XXXI.

fered from states of excitement during which she presented an exquisitely childish and silly behavior. This happened regularly whenever she was forced to repress sad thought-complexes: Janet is acquainted with this behavior which naturally appears in all gradations. He says: " These persons play a sort of comedy, they are young, naive, coaxing, they pretend complete ignorance and get to be quite like little children." (" Obsessions," p. 391.)

3. INTELLECTUAL DISTURBANCES.

Consciousness in dementia præcox shows anomalies which have in many ways been compared to those of hysteria and hypnotism. Often there exist signs of narrowing of consciousness, that is, there is diminished clearness of one idea with abnormal increase of unclearness in all by-associations. Conforming to the views of various authors we may thus explain blind acceptance of ideas without inhibition or correction, a thing analogous to suggestion. Many would explain the peculiar suggestibility of catatonics (echo symptoms) on this basis. The only objection to be advanced against this view is the fact that there is considerable difference between normal and catatonic suggestibility. Normally we observe that the subject will, if possible, accurately adhere to the suggestion if he attempts to realize it, whereas in hysteria peculiar modifications may take place corresponding to the degree and kind of the disease. A suggested sleep may easily transform itself into a hysterohypnosis or into a hysterical dream-state, or the suggestions are only partially executed by the addition of unintentional by-actions.[9] It is for this reason that hypnosis is less controllable in pronounced hysterics than in normal persons. The accidental in the suggestive manifestations of

[9] For some time I treated a hysterical patient who suffered from intense depression, headaches, and total inability to work. Whenever I suggested to her to find pleasure in work and to be more cheerful, she was, on the following day often abnormally happy, laughed incessantly, and had a strong impulse to work so that she worked till late in the night. On the third day she was profoundly exhausted. The happy disposition appearing without any motive was unpleasant to her because she constantly thought of nonsense and silly jokes, and laughed impulsively.

An example of hystero-hypnosis can be found in my work, Ein Fall von hysterischem Stupor bei einer Untersuchungsgefangenen. Journ. f. Psych. u. Neur., 1902.

catatonics is still greater. Suggestibility often limits itself entirely to a motor sphere, resulting only in an echopraxia and often only in an echolalia. Verbal suggestion can rarely be carried out in dementia præcox, and even if it succeeds the effects are uncontrollable and as if accidental. There are always a number of strange elements mixed together with the normal suggestibility in dementia præcox. Nevertheless there is no reason why catatonic suggestibility, at least in its normal remnants, could not be reduced to the same psychological mechanism as in hysteria. We know that in hysteria the uncontrollable part of the suggestive effects is to be sought for in the autonomous complexes, and there is nothing against this being the case in dementia præcox. A capricious behavior similar to the one shown in suggestion is seen in dementia præcox in relation to other psycho-therapeutic measures, such as transfer, discharge,[10] education by example, etc. That improvement in old catatonics when transferred to new suf-roundings depends on psychological causes is shown by the fine and very valuable analyses of Riklin.[11]

The lucidity of consciousness in dementia præcox is subject to all possible forms of obscuration; it may change from perfect clearness to the deepest confusion. Through Janet we know that in hysteria the fluctuation of lucidity is almost proverbial. In hysteria we are able to distinguish two kinds of disturbances, momentary and persisting. The momentary disturbance may be a slight *"engourdissement"* of a few seconds duration, or it may be a momentary hallucinatory and ecstatic invasion likewise of very short duration. In dementia præcox we know the abrupt obstructions, the momentary "thought-deprivation," and the lightning-like hallucinatory incursions with bizarre impulses. The lasting disturbance of lucidity in hysteria we know in the form of somnambulistic states with numerous hallucinations or in the form of " lethargic " (Löwenfeld) or cataleptic conditions. In dementia præcox it is shown in the form of persisting hallucinatory phases with more or less marked confusion and in stuporous states.

Attention in dementia præcox is, so to say, regularly disturbed, but the same disorder also plays a great part in the realms of

---

[10] See Bleuler: Frühe Entlassungen. Psych. Neur. Wochenschr., 1905.
[11] Über Versetzungsbesserungen. Psychiatr. Neurol. Wochenschr., 1905.

hysteria. Janet notes the following as to the "*troubles de l'attention*": "One can say that the main trouble exists not only in a suppression of the intellectual faculties, but in the difficulty of fixing the attention. Their mind is always distracted by some vague preoccupation and they never give themselves up entirely to the object which one assigns to them." As shown in the first chapter, the words of Janet may also be applied to dementia præcox. It is the autonomous complex which disturbs the concentration of the patients, it paralyzes all other psychic activities, a fact which curiously escaped Janet. What is striking in hysteria (just as in other affective states) is the fact that the patients always return to their "stories" (as in traumatic hysteria!) and that all their thoughts and actions are constellated by the complex only. A similar narrow-mindedness, but of the highest intensity, we frequently observe in dementia præcox, especially in the paranoid form. It is hardly necessary to give examples. Orientation in both diseases changes in a similar capricious manner. In dementia præcox, where one is not actually dealing with marked excitability and deep confusion, we often get the impression that the patients are only disturbed by illusions, but that in reality they are properly oriented. In hysteria we do not always receive the same impression, but we may convince ourselves that proper orientation exists by hypnotizing the patient. Hypnosis represses the hysterical complex and allows a reproduction of the ego-complex. As in hysteria, disorientation is due to the fact that some pathogenic complex pushes the ego-complex away from the reproduction, a thing which may happen instantaneously; likewise in dementia præcox it may readily happen that quite clear answers are often replaced at the very next moment by the most singular utterances.[12] The lucidity of consciousness is especially

---

[12] A nice example of momentary variations in hysteria is found in the work of Riklin: Über den Ganserschen Symptomencomplex. Psych. neur. Wochenschr., 1904. He shows that a patient manifested correct or delusional orientation depending on the manner of questioning. The same thing can happen spontaneously when the complex is excited by a stimulus. Riklin reports a corresponding experimental case in Cont. VII of the Diag. Assoz.-Stud. where at a critical stimulus word a dreamy state occurred and held on for some time. The pathological fancies are principally the same thing, as *e. g.*, the automatic insertions in the language or writing in somnambulism (See Flournoy).

injured in the acute stages where the patients often are in a real dream,[13] that is, in a " complex-delirium."[14]

The hallucinatory delirious phases may, as we have said, be placed parallel to hysteria (of course it must always be kept in mind that we deal with two different diseases). The content of the hysterical delirium, as we readily discover when we use Freud's method of analysis, is always a clear complex-delirium; that is, the pathogenic complex appears as self-acting and spends its vitality usually in the form of wish-realization.[15]

In the corresponding acute phases of dementia præcox we do not have to look long in order to find similar things. Every psychiatrist knows the deliria of unmarried women who pass through betrothals, marriages, coitus, pregnancies and births. I content myself here with this allusion, reserving everything till later, when I shall return to these questions. They are of extraordinary importance for the determination of the symptoms.[16]

[13] See E. Meyer: Beitrag zur Kenntnis der akut entstandenen Psychosen. Berlin, 1899.

[14] I recall the fact that a normal dream is always a " complex-delirium"; i. e., its content is determined by one or more complexes which are actual. Freud as we know has shown this. If one analyses his dreams by the Freud method he immediately sees the justification for the expression "complex-delirium." A great many dreams are wish fulfilments. Endogenous dreams exclusively concern complexes while exogenous ones; i. e., those influenced or produced during sleep by physical stimuli are as far as I have observed until now, blendings of complex constellations with more or less symbolic elaboration of bodily sensations.

[15] Ganser's dreamy states and the deliria of somnambulists furnish good examples. Comp. Riklin: Psych.-Neur. Wochenschr., 1904. Jung, Jour. f. Psych. u. Neur., 1902 u. 1903. A fine example of complex-delirium with misinterpretations is given by Weiskorn: A twenty-one year old primipara refers to her labor pains as follows; grasping her abdomen she asks: " Who presses me here?" The descent of the caput she refers to as a hard passage of the bowels. Transitorische Geistesstörungen beim Geburtsakt., Diss., Bonn, 1897. v. Krafft-Ebing reports transparent deliria, Lehbr. and C. Meyer in Jahrb. f. Psych., XI, p. 236. Clear complex-deliria are the semi or unconscious fanciful creations of the hysterics described by Pick (Jahrb. f. Psych. u. Neur., XIV, p. 280) as well as the romances of Helene Smith described by Flournoy and the somnambulists observed by me. Another clear case is found by Bohn (Ein Fall von doppeltem Bewusstsein, Dissert., Breslau, 1898).

[16] Riklin in his works on Versetsungsbesserungen has already given some contributions worth mentioning (Psych. Neur. Wochenschr., 1905). As

We pass then to the realm of delusions and hallucinations. Both symptoms occur in all mental diseases and also in hysteria. One therefore deals with mechanisms which are universally formed and are set free by the most variable injuries. What chiefly interests us is the content of the delusions and hallucinations to which we may also add the pathological fancies. Here, too, hysteria, this most transparent disease, can help us. Obsessive ideas can be placed parallel to delusions; so may also the affective narrow-minded prejudices which are so often met with in hysteria, and the stubbornly asserted bodily pains and complaints. I cannot repeat the genesis of these hysterical and delusional assertions, I must presuppose a knowledge of Freud's investigations. The delusional assertions of the hysteric are transferences, that is, the accompanying affect does not belong to them but to a repressed complex, which is veiled in this manner. An indomitable obsessive idea only goes to show that a complex (generally sexual) is repressed; the same is true of the other stubbornly asserted hysterical symptoms. We now have a well-grounded hypothesis (I base this on many dozens of analyses), that an undoubtedly similar process exists in the delusional

an example I cite one of his cases: Miss M. S. twenty-six years old, educated and intelligent, six years ago passed through a brief psychosis, but has so well recovered that she was discharged as cured and the diagnosis of dementia præcox was not made. Before the present attack she fell in love with a composer from whom she took singing lessons. Her love soon reached a passionate height accompanied by periods of insane excitement. She was then brought to the Burghölzli asylum. At first she looked upon her confinement and her new experiences in the asylum as a descent into the underworld. She got this idea from her teacher's last composition which was "Charon." Then after this purifying passage through the underworld she interpreted everything happening about her in the sense of vicissitudes and struggles which she had to undergo in order to become united with her lover. Patient then considered another patient as being her lover and for a couple of nights went into her bed. She then thought herself pregnant, felt and heard twins in her womb, a girl resembling herself and a boy resembling the father. Later she thought that she gave birth to a child and had hallucinations of having a child in bed. With this the psychosis came to a close. She had found a solacing substitute for reality. She soon became quiet, her behavior freer, the rigidity in her attitude and gait disappeared and she readily gave catamnestic information, so that her statements could be well compared with those in the hospital records.

system of dementia præcox.[17]   To illustrate my view I will cite this simple example.

A thirty-two-year-old servant had her teeth extracted so as to have a complete new set inserted. During the night following the operation there appeared a marked condition of anxiety. She considered herself damned and lost forever because she had committed a great sin. She should not have had her teeth extracted. People should pray for her that God might forgive her sins. The following morning the patient was again quiet and continned her work, but during the succeeding nights the anxiousness increased. I investigated her antecedent history obtained from her employers in whose service she had been for a number of years. Nothing, however, was known and the patient denied any kind of emotivity in her former life and emphasized with great affect that the extraction of the teeth was the cause of her disease. The disease rapidly progressed and the patient, manifesting all the symptoms of catatonia, had to be committed. Then it was discovered that for many years she had been concealing an illegitimate child, of whose existence even her family had not the slightest knowledge. For a year past the patient had been acquainted with a man whom she wished to marry, but could not fully decide to do so, as she was constantly worried by the fear that her lover would cast her off on learning of her former life. Here, then, was the source of the anxiety, and at the same time it becomes clear why the affect was inadequate to the extraction of the teeth.

The mechanism of transference shows the way to the comprehension of the origin of a delusional assertion. This way, however, is made difficult on account of infinite impediments. The well known oddness of the delusions in dementia præcox barely admits of any analogies. Nevertheless we have essential facts in normal as well as in hysterical psychology to allow of at least approaching the most familiar delusional forms.

[17] Godfernaux in his psychological analysis of Magnan's *délere chronique à évolution systématique* finds at its base mostly an effective disturbance: "In reality the thought of the patient is passive; he orients himself without taking into account all of his conceptions in the direction prescribed by his affective state."
Le sentiment et la pensée, p. 8.

Delusions of reference have been thoroughly analyzed and explained by Bleuler.[18] Feelings of reference are found where there is a markedly accentuated complex. It is the peculiarity of all strong complexes to assimilate as much as possible; it is also a known fact that at the time of a strong affect we often have a momentary feeling as if "some one noticed it." An acute affect will especially cause assimilations of quite indifferent occurrences from the environment and thus the coarsest errors of judgment result. When we meet with some mishap we are quite ready during our first outbursts of anger to assume that someone intentionally injured and insulted us. In hysteria such prejudice may establish itself for a long time, corresponding to the magnitude and duration of the affect, and through which, without anything further, slight delusions of reference result. From this to the delusional assumption of strange machinations is only a step. This road leads to paranoia.[19] The incredible and grotesque delusions of dementia præcox are frequently with difficulty explained by the delusions of reference. If, for example, a precocious dement perceives everything taking place within and without him as unnatural and "concocted," we may assume a stronger disturbance than delusions of reference.[20] There is evidently something in the apperception of dementia præcox which prevents normal assimilation. The apperception either lacks a nuance or possesses one too much, thus receiving a strange accentuation (Berze!). In the hysterical realms we find analogies to this in disturbances of the feelings of activity. Every psychic activity, aside from the tone of pleasure and pain, is accompanied by still another feeling-tone which qualifies it in its own particular way (Höffding). What we mean by this will be best explained by the important observations of Janet in psychasthenics. The

---

[18] Affektivität, etc. Compare also Neisser: Allg. Ztschr. f. Psych., Bd. LIII.

[19] Compare Marguliés: Monatschr. f. Psych. u. Neur., Bd. X, and Gierlich: Arch. f. Psych., Bd. XL. See Nervous and Mental Disease Monograph Series No. 2, Studies in Paranoia, for a translation of Gierlich's article.

[20] A precocious dement under my care finds everything artificial; what the doctor tells him, what the other patients do, the cleaning in the ward, the food, etc., all are artificial. It is all done by "one of his persecutors" who has a princess "by the head and thus blabs to the people what they are to do."

decisions of volition and action are not accompanied by the same feeling as under normal conditions, but, for example, by "*senti-ments d'incomplétude*": "The subject feels that the action is not completely finished, that something is lacking."[21] Or every decision of volition is accompanied by a "*sentiment d'incapacité*": "These persons from the beginning experience painful feelings in the thought that it is necessary to act; they fear action above all things. Their dream, as they all say, is of a life where there will be nothing more to do."[22] A most important abnormity of the feeling of activity in dementia præcox is the "*sentiment d'automatisme.*"[23] A patient expresses himself about it as follows: "I am unable to give an account of what I really do, everything is mechanical in me and is done unconsciously, I am only a machine."[24]

Closely related to it is the "*sentiment de domination.*"[25] A patient describes this feeling as follows: "For four months I have had queer ideas; it seems to me that I am obliged to think and say them; someone makes me speak, someone suggests to me coarse words and it is not my fault if my mouth works in spite of me."

A precocious dement might talk in a similar manner. Hence one may be allowed to question whether we are not here dealing with dementia præcox. I carefully examined the lectures of Janet[26] in order to see whether or not among his pathological material there were cases of dementia præcox. This might be quite possible in the works of French authors. But I found nothing that would point to the fact that the above cited patient was a case of dementia præcox. Moreover, we frequently hear such utterances from hysterics and somnambulists, and finally we hear similar expressions among many normal persons who are under the domination of an unusually strong complex, like poets and artists (see for example what Nietzsche says about the origin of Zarathustra).[27] A good example of disturbance of

[21] Obsessions et Psychasthénie, V. I, p. 264.
[22] *L. c.,* p. 266.
[23] *L. c.,* p. 272.
[24] Comp. Ball, Revue scientifique, 1882, II, 43.
[25] Janet, *l. c.,* p. 273.
[26] Works, Vol. VI, p. 482.
[27] Works, Vol. VI, p. 482.

feeling of activity is the "*sentiment de perception incomplète.*"[28] A patient says: "It is as though I see things through a veil, a mist, or through a wall which separates me from reality." A normal person who is under the immediate influence of a great affect might express himself in a similar manner. But precocions dements express themselves in a like manner when they speak about their indefinite perception of the environment ("It seems to me as if you are the doctor," "they say it was my mother," "it looks like Burghölzli, but it is not").[29] The expression of Janet's patient, "The world appears to me like a gigantic hallucination," is true in the fullest sense also of precocious dements who always (especially in the acute stages) live, so to say, as in a dream, and they express themselves in a corresponding manner both during the disease and catamnestically.

The "*sentiments d'incomplétude*" are also especially related to the affects. A patient of Janet said: "It seems to me that I will not see my children again; everything leaves me indifferent and cold and I wish I could despair, cry out from pain; I know that I ought to be unhappy, but I do not arrive at that state; I have no more pleasure than pain; I know that a repast is good but I swallow it because it is necessary without finding in it the pleasure that I would have found before. There is an enormous thickness preventing me from feeling the moral impressions." Another patient says: "I would like to try to think of my little girl but I can not, the thought of my child barely passes through my mind and does not leave me any feeling."

I have repeatedly heard similar spontaneous utterances from hysterics as well as from precocious dements who were still able to give more or less information. A young catatonic woman who was forced to part from her husband and child under especially tragic circumstances, showed a total lack of emotion for all familiar reminiscences. I placed before her the whole very sad situation, and attempted to evoke an adequate feeling. While I spoke she laughed, when I finished she became calm for a moment and said, "I simply can not feel any more."

According to our conception, the "*sentiments d'incomplétude,*" etc., are products of inhibition which emanate from an over-

[28] Janet, *l. c.,* p. 282.
[29] Excellent examples can also be found in Shreber's, Denkwürdigkeiten.

whelming complex. Whenever we are dominated by a complex it is only the ideas belonging to it which possess a full tone, that is, they alone possess perfect clearness, all other perceptions originating either from within or without are subject to an inhibition, through which they become indistinct, that is, they lose some feeling-tone. This is the basis for the resulting imperfection of the feeling of activity and finally for the want of emotion. These disturbances alone condition the feeling of strangeness. The reasoning faculty which is preserved in hysteria prevents the immediate outward projection as happens in dementia præcox. But if we by judgment facilitate the outward projection by allowing some superstitious ideas to creep in, there soon result explanations in the sense of a power coming from without. The clearest examples are given by the spirit mediums where a mass of insignificant things are referred to as transcendental causes; of course, it must be said that they are never as awkward and grotesque as in dementia præcox. We see something similar in normal dreams where there is outward projection with absolute certainty and ingenuousness. The psychological mechanisms of dreams and hysteria are most closely related to those of dementia preæcox. A comparison with dreams is therefore not too daring. In dreams we see how reality is spun with fanciful creations, how the pale memory pictures of the waking state assume tangible forms, and how the impressions of the environment adapt themselves to the sense of the dream. The dreamer finds himself in a new and different world which he has projected out of himself. Let the dreamer walk about and act like one awakened and we have the clinical picture of dementia præcox.

I am unable to discuss here in detail all delusions. I should like, however, to discuss briefly the well known delusions of influence. The idea of influencing of thought occurs in many forms, the most frequent being that of "thought-deprivation." The patients often complain that their thought is taken away[30] whenever they wish to think or say something.[31]

[30] An original form of thought-deprivation is reported by Klinke: "A patient's thoughts are made to come out by the passing to and fro of the other patients in the ward."

[31] Also in hysterics these manifestations are not at all rare, as I have observed. Janet calls them "*eclipses mentales*" (T. complains of often feeling a singular arrest of her thought, she loses her ideas), *l. c.*, p. 369.

By the method of outward projection they frequently place the responsibility on some foreign agency. Externally "thought_ deprivation" is manifested in the form of "obstructions."[32] The examiner suddenly receives no answer to his questions and the patient then states that he is unable to answer as his thoughts were "taken away." The association experiments taught us that long reaction times and incorrect reactions ("mistakes") regularly appear where one deals with a complex-reaction. The strong feeling-tone inhibits the associations. This phenomenon more intensified is also found in hysteria where at critical points the patient "can simply think of nothing." This is almost thought-deprivation. The same mechanism is found in dementia præcox; here too thought is inhibited at complex-locations (be it in experiments or conversation). This can easily be seen in suitable cases when we at first speak about matters indifferent to the patient and later about things referring to the complexes. With the indifferent material the answers follow smoothly, while with the complexes one obstruction succeeds the other; the patients either refuse to answer or give deliberately affected evasions. Thus, no matter how patiently one tries, it is impossible to obtain detailed statements from a patient about her husband with whom she has lived unhappily, whereas about anything else she gives ready and detailed information.

Another phenomenon to be considered is impulsive thought. Singular and even senseless ideas crowd themselves into a patient's mind, about which he is obsessively forced to deliberate and ponder. An analogy to this we find in psychogenic obsessive thoughts. The patients regularly realize the absurdity of the thoughts, but are unable to repress them.[33] The thought influences also manifest themselves as "inspirations."

[32] "Theories," like those, for instance, of Rogues de Fursac, only verify the fact. "The most suitable term is perhaps that of psychic interference. The two opposed tendencies annul each other, as contrary waves do in physics." (Cited after Claus: Catatonie et Stupeur, Bruxelles, 1903.) See also Mendel: Leitfaden der Psych., p. 55.

[33] An analogy of this is Janet's "*rêverie forcée*" in his "Obsédés," *l. c.*, p. 154: "J. feels that at certain moments all his life concentrates itself into his head, that the rest of his body is as if asleep, and that he is forced to think enormously without being able to stop himself. The memory becomes extraordinarily and excessively developed so that it

That we have here a phenomenon which does not exclusively limit itself to dementia præcox is already shown by the word " inspiration," which designates a psychic event appearing wherever there exists an autonomous complex. We deal here with sudden invasions of complexes into consciousness. Inspirations are not at all unusual in religious people. The modern protestant theologians have gone so far as to call it " inner experiences." " Inspirations " are an every-day occurrence in somnambulism.

Finally we have another form of obstruction, " fascination " (an expression coined by one of my female patients). Sommer described this phenomenon as " optical fixation." We observe " fascination " in association experiments even outside of dementia præcox, especially in conditions of emotional stupidity. This condition may be evoked under circumstances by an experiment or through a complex stimulated during the experiment. The patients then begin to react (at least for a time) not to the stimulus word, but they simply name objects from the surroundings. I have especially noticed this in imbeciles, in normal persons during a strong affect, in hysterics at complex-locations and in dementia præcox.

" Fascination " is distraction to the environment in order to conceal the vacuum of inner associations or the complex producing the vacuum. It is the same in principle as breaking away from an unpleasant conversation by sudden diversion to some remote banality. As a starting point any object of the environment serves. We have therefore enough evidence to enable us to place the mechanism of " fascination " on a parallel with the normal.

Experience shows that all these disturbances appear in dementia præcox about the complex and belong to the measures of defense. Here we are also obliged to discuss negativism. The prototype of negativism is " obstruction " which, in some cases, gives the impression of an intentional refusal, just as the " I don't know " of hysterics. One can just as well speak of negativism when the patients refuse to answer questions. The passive negativism readily becomes active, whereby the patients also psychically defend themselves against the examination. If we exclude these cases where the negativism has generalized

is impossible to direct it by attention." Compare also the case in Beitrag VI of Diag. Assoz. Stud.

itself into a common state of defense, we find that in the still accessible cases the negativism as well as the obstructions are at complex-locations. As soon as the association experiment or the examination strikes the complex, that is, the tender spot, the patient refuses to answer and retreats, just as the hysteric uses all sorts of pretexts in order to conceal the complex. How great an inclination the catatonic symptoms have towards generalization is particularly shown in negativism. Whereas in hysteria, in spite of a repeatedly very strong and impeding negativism, we still find certain accessible tracts to the mind, the negativistic catatonic shuts himself in completely, so that at least for the moment there are. no means of penetrating. Occasionally the negativism is called forth by a single critical question. A special form of negativism is the evasive speaking, which we know in a similar form in the Ganser symptom-complex. Here, just as there, one deals with a more or less unconscious refusal to enter into conversation, hence something similar to the fascination and thought-deprivation. The Ganser symptom-complex, as was shown by Riklin's and my own works, has its own good reasons ; the patients wish to repress their complex. In dementia præcox it is probably due to the same thing. In the psychoanalysis of hysteria we regularly find that the by-speaking or circumlocution occurs at the complex ; the same is found at the complexes of de-mentia præcox, only that here this symptom, as well as all the catatonic symptoms, show a tendency to generalization. The catatonic symptoms of the motor spheres can be conceived with-out any difficulty as radiating effects of generalization. This is probably true in the majority of cases. It is true, however, that catatonic symptoms appear in localized and general brain dis-turbances where one cannot very well think of a psychological nexus. But here we also see at least just as frequently hysterical manifestations, whose psychogenesis is otherwise an established fact. What we should learn from this is never to forget the pos-sibility of thinking " the other way."

An hallucination is crudely an outward projection of a psychic element. Clinically we know all gradations from inspiration or pathological fancy to loud hallucinations of hearing or to plastic vision. Hallucinations are ubiquitous. Dementia præcox only sets in motion a preformed mechanism which normally regularly functionates in dreams. The hallucinations of hysteria, just as those of dreams, contain symbolically disfigured complex fragments. This also holds true[34] of most of the hallucinations of dementia præcox, only that here they are pushed still further and are of a more dreamlike disfigurement. Disfigurements of speech, after the example of dream-paraphasias (comp. Freud, Stransky and Kraepelin), are extraordinarily frequent; most of them are contaminations. A patient who entertained delusions of sin, noticing a Japanese in the clinic, heard the voices call out " Japansinner " (Japansünder). It is remarkable that not a few patients who tend to form numerous neologisms and peculiar delusions, that is, who are under the complete domination of the complex, are often corrected by the voices. One of my patients, for example, was twitted by the voices about her grandiose delusions, or the voices commanded the patient to tell the physician who was occupying himself with her delusions that " he should not bother himself with these things." Another patient who has been in the hospital for a number of years and always speaks in a disdainful manner about his own family is told by the voices that " he is homesick." From this and numerous other examples I received the impression that the correcting voices are perhaps invasions of the repressed normal remnant of the ego-complex. That the normal ego-complex does not entirely perish, but is prevented from reproduction by the disease-complex, seems to me to be shown by the fact that during severe physical diseases or any other deep-going changes, the patients suddenly begin to react in a tolerably normal manner.[35] Sleep disturb-

[34] During the absence of her fiancé a girl was seduced. She concealed it from her fiancé. More than ten years later she was afflicted with dementia præcox. The disease began by feeling that people entertained suspicions against her morality, and that she heard voices talking about her secret, which finally compelled her to make a confession to her husband.

Many patients state directly that the " sin register " is read for them with all its details and that voices " know everything " and take it up with them. It would therefore seem very strange that most of the patients are unable to give satisfactory information about their hallucinations. It is due here to the reproduction of the complexes which, as we have seen, are under special inhibitions.

[35] A patient who was quite inaccessible and who always greeted the doctors in the most scurrilous manner fell ill with a grave gastro-

ances are quite usual in dementia præcox and manifest themselves in a manifold manner. The dreams are often very vivid and we can readily understand that frequently patients are unable to properly correct them. Many patients draw their delusions exclusively from the dreams to which they attribute real validity.[36] The part played by the vivid dreams of hysteria is well known. Besides disturbances by dreams, many other complex-fragments may disturb sleep, such as hallucinations, fancies, etc., just as hypnosis does in hysteria. Frequently patients complain about their unnatural sleep, which is not at all a real sleep, but an artificial rigidity. We hear similar complaints wherever there exists a strong affect which cannot be totally extinguished by sleep-inhibition and therefore accompanies sleep as a constant keynote (e. g., melancholia and depressive affects in hysteria). Not seldom intelligent hysterics feel the " complex-restlessness " in their sleep and can precisely detail it. A patient of Janet says: " There are always two or three of my personalities who do not sleep, nevertheless I have fewer personalities during sleep; there are some who sleep but little. These persons dream, but not the same dream. I feel that there are some who dream of different things." With these remarks the patient nicely expresses the feeling of the unrelenting and laboring autonomous complex which does not surrender to the sleep-inhibition of the ego-complex.

enteritis. With the onset of the disease he became completely changed, he was patient and grateful, obeyed all requests and always gave polite and precise information. His convalescence manifested itself by his again becoming monosyllabic and shut in, and one fine morning he signalled his complete recovery by receiving the doctor with the following: " Here comes again one of the flock of dogs and apes who wishes to play the Saviour."

[36] Compare Sante de Sanctis: Die Träume, Halle, 1901, and Kazowsky: Neuro. Zentr.-Bl., 1901, p. 440.

We have a patient who entertains the most manifold sexual delusions which exclusively originate from dreams, as we were able to convince ourselves on numerous occasions. Patient simply takes the contents of her dreams which are all very vivid and plastic, as real, and corresponding to the dream she becomes abusive, querulous and complaining, but only in writing. In her general behavior she is nice and orderly in contradistinction to the contents of her letters and writings.

4. STEREOTYPY.

By stereotypy in its broadest sense we understand the persistent and constant reproduction of certain activities, such as verbigeration, catalepsy, persistent phrases, perseverations, etc. These manifestations belong to the most characteristic symptoms of dementia præcox. Yet stereotypy in the form of automatization is also one of the most usual manifestations in the development of the normal psyche (Spencer). All our abilities and the whole progress of our personality rest on automatization. The process leading to it is the following: In order to perform a certain activity we direct all our attention on the appertaining ideas and through this markedly accentuated tone we engrave the phases of the process into memory. The effect of frequent repetitions causes a " smoother " path, upon which the activity finally moves automatically almost without our aid. Only a slight impulse is necessary to immediately put the mechanism in motion. The same thing may take place in us passively through strong affects. We can be forced to certain action by affects; at first there is great inhibition, but later, on account of numerous repetitions of the affect, the inhibition becomes less and finally the reaction succeeds promptly even on a very slight impulse. This can especially be observed in the bad habits of children.

The strong feeling-tone creates tracks, whereby we again express the same things that we have said of the complex: Every complex has a tendency to autonomy and to independent living; it has a greater tendency to persist and to reproduction than indifferent thought; it has therefore the best prospect for becoming automatic. Hence if anything becomes automatic in the mind an antecedent feeling-tone must always be postulated for it.[37] This is most clearly seen in hysteria, where we are able to trace all stereotypies (like convulsive attacks), absences, complaints and symptoms, to the underlying affects. In normal association experiments we find so-called perseverations regularly at complex-locations.[38]

[37] As previously stated attention belongs under the collective idea of Gefühlston (feeling tone).
[38] Occasionally the complex-content continues to persevere. In the majority of cases, however, there exists only one persevering disturbance which may perhaps be ascribed to the fact that the complex through dis-

If a strong complex exists, there results a cessation of progress adapted to the environment, and associations gyrate altogether about the complex. This is generally so in hysteria where we meet the strongest complexes. The progress of personality is suspended and a great part of the psychic activity is spent in dressing the complex in every possible form (symptom-actions). It is not in vain that Janet calls attention to the general disturbances of the " *obsédé*," of which I will mention the following: " *l'indolence, l'irrésolution, les retards, la fatigue, l'inachèvement, l'aboulie, l'inhibition*, etc."[39] If a complex succeeds in fixing itself, monotony results, especially the monotony of external symptoms. Who does not know the stereotyped and tiring complaints of hysterics? the obstinacy and invincibility of their symptoms? Just as a constant pain will always call forth the same monotonous plaintive sounds, so will a fixed complex gradnally stereotype the whole mode of speech of the individual, so that we can finally know that day after day we will receive with mathematical accuracy the same answer to a certain question.

In these processes we find some of the normal prototypes for the stereotypy of dementia præcox.[40] When we examine the

traction leaves an association-vacuum. This similarity occurs in the distraction experiments where, on account of a vacuum of association, one despairingly resorts to antecedent associations. If, however, as in the cases of Heilbronner, somewhat more difficult questions are given, it may result in an emotion and serves the same purpose as a complex. The association-vacuum is primary, inasmuch as there exist no fluent associations to the stimulus ideas in question. In the normal it is the complex which mostly perseveres.

[39] Janet, *l. c.*, p. 335 ff., p. 349, says: "This more or less complete stoppage of certain actions is one of the most essential phenomena in the mental states of the obsessed" (p. 105). "These forced operations are not normal. They are the operations of thought, of action, and of emotion, which are at once excessive, sterile, and of inferior kind."

[40] Pfister (Uber Verbigeration. Vortrag auf der Versammlung des Deutsch. Ver. f. Psychiatrie in München, 1906. Ref. Neurol.-Psychiatr. Wochenschr., No. 7, 1906) asks whether the stereotypies or the verbigerations have psychological motives or not. He however leaves the question open. Pfister seems to be of the same opinion as we; that each stereotypy has an ideational content as its basis, which, however, on account of its morbidly disturbed manner of expression manifests itself in a distorted manner. ("It is conceivable that ideation stereotypies have an impulse to express themselves, but in their places there is a reproduction

origin of linguistic or mimic stereotypies, we often find the associated emotional content. Later the content always becomes more indistinct just as in the normal or in the hysterical automatism. But in dementia præcox the corresponding process seems to run a more rapid and thorough course, so that one soon reaches the vacuum as regards content and emotion.

As experience undoubtedly teaches, it is not only the complex-content that becomes stereotyped in dementia præcox, but also accidental material. It is known that the verbigerating patients will take up an accidental stray word and repeat it constantly. Heilbronner, Stransky and others justly interpret such phenomena as symptoms of association-vacuums. The motility stereotypies can also be easily interpreted in the same manner. We know that precocious dements suffer very frequently from associative obstructions ("thought-deprivation"). This disappearance of thought is found by preference around the complex. If then the complex plays the enormous rôle entrusted to it, it is to be expected that it very frequently absorbs many thoughts, and in this way disturbs the *fonction du réel.* In the place of the alienated realms it creates association-vacuums and those phenomena of perseveration which may be explained by the "vacuum."

It is a characteristic of most of the ontogenetically acquired automatisms that they are subjected to gradual changes. The anamneses of Tiquers (see Meige et Feindel, "Le Tic") afford many proofs of that. The catatonic automatisms are no exceptions, they too change slowly, frequently the transformation

of senseless phrases and neologisms. This is due to the simultaneous existence of the decaying and exciting processes in the central apparatus of speech which make their clear manifestation impossible, and instead of stereotyped thoughts [as results of paralogic-paraphasic malformations] only unintelligible remnants come to view.") There is still another way in which the decay of speech can undermine the manifestations of correct ideation stereotypies, and that is, that (on account of the disturbances in the recoinage of ideas and thoughts both in word and speech) through the monotonous repetition of ideas no equivalent speech formation can be incited. In the conversion of thought to expression of speech, numerous paralogic derailments occur, the presentations become erroneously associated, changing everywhere, so that, forthwith, in place of the thought stereotypy which remains hidden, there is a reproduction of constantly·changing nonsense.

process taking years. The following examples will show what
I mean.

A catatonic sang persistently for hours a religious song with
the refrain " Hallelujah." Then she began to verbigerate for
hours " Hallelujah," which gradually degenerated into " hallo,"
" oha," and finally she verbigerated " ha—ha—ha " accompanied
by convulsive laughter.

In the year 1900 a patient combed his head a few hours every
day in a stereotyped manner, so as to remove the " gypsum "
which " was smeared into the hair " during the night. The following year he gradually stopped using the comb on his head.
In 1903 the patient beat and scraped his chest with it, and at
present he has reached the inguinal region.

In quite a similar manner the voices and delusions degenerate.[41]
In a like manner the " word-salad " originates. The original
simple sentences become more and more complicated with neologisms, they are constantly loudly or quietly verbigerated and
gradually become blurred, so that an unintelligible medley results
which probably sounds similar to the " stupid chattering " with
which many patients are affected.

A patient under my observation during convalescence from
acute dementia præcox begins quietly to relate to herself how she
packs her trunk, goes from the ward to the asylum gate, then
to the street, and then to the railroad station; how she gets
into the train and reaches her home, where her wedding is solem-
nized, etc. This story became more and more stereotyped, the
individual halting places became mixed without any order, the
sentences became imperfect, some were abbreviated to a single
catch-word, and now after more than a year the patient only
occasionally uses a catch-word; all other words she has replaced
by " hm—hm—hm— " which she utters in a stereotyped manner
with the same tone and rhythm as when she formerly told her
story. At times when she becomes excited the former sentences
reappear. We also know from hallucinatory patients that the
voices in time become emptier and quieter, but when they become
excited the voices regain in content and distinctness.

[41] Compare especially Schreber: Denkwürdigkeiten. Schreber describes
very well how the contents of the auditory hallucinations become gram-
matically abbreviated.

These gradually creeping changes are very distinctly seen in obsessive ideas (see Cont. VIII). Janet, too, speaks of the gradual changes of obsessive processes.[42]

There are, however, stereotypies or rather stereotyped automatisms which from the very beginning do not show any psychic content by which they can be understood even symbolically. I am thinking especially now of the almost muscular manifestations of automatism, like catalepsy, or certain forms of negativistic muscular resistances. These exquisite catatonic symptoms, as has been already shown by many investigators, we also find in organic disturbances, such as paralysis, brain tumors, etc. Brain physiology, especially the well-known experiments of Goltz, teach that in vertebrates when the cerebrum is removed a condition of automatism par excellence results. Forel's experiments with ants (destroying the corpora quadrigemina) shows that automatism results when the greatest (and most differentiated?) part of brain tissue is removed. The debrained animal becomes the well-known "reflex machine," it remains either sitting or standing in a certain preferred attitude until it is forced by external stimuli to a reflex action. It is certainly a somewhat daring analogy when some cases of catatonia are compared to such reflex machines, although they frequently appeal to one as such. But when we go somewhat deeper and consider that in this disease a complex occupies almost all the associations, holding them persistently, that this complex is absolutely unassailable by psychological stimuli, that it is, as it were, split off from all external influences, it would then seem that the before mentioned analogy is of somewhat greater significance. The complex on account of its intensity lays claim to the brain activity in its greatest extent, so that a great number of impulses belonging to other spheres become dissipated. It can then be easily understood that on account of the predominance, the congealing of a complex, a con-

---

[42] Janet, l. c., p. 125. A female patient says: "Formerly I used to look back in memory in order to know whether I ought to reproach myself for something, in order to reassure myself about my conduct—but now it is not at all the same thing. I always recall what I have done a week or two weeks ago, and I see the things exactly, but I have absolutely no interest in seeing them."

In this example the deviation from the content proper is especially noteworthy.

dition will result in the brain which functionally at least will be more or less equal to a destruction of a great part of the brain. To be sure this hypothesis cannot be proven any further, but it may explain many things not reached by psychological analysis.

Summary.

Hysteria contains in its innermost essence a complex which could never be totally overcome; in a measure the psyche is brought to a standstill since it is unable to rid itself of the complex. Most of the associations go in the direction of the complex, and the chief function of psychic activity is to elaborate the complex in every possible direction. For this reason (in chronic stages) the individual is forced to retire more and more from an adaptation to the environment. The wish-dreams and wish-deliria of hysteria occupy themselves exclusively with the fulfilment of the wish-complex. Many hysterics succeed, after a time, in regaining equilibrium by conquering the complex and by avoiding new traumas.

In dementia præcox we likewise find one or more complexes which become tenaciously fixed. Here, too, we have complexes which can no longer be conquered. Whereas in hysteria there exists an unmistakable causal relation between the complex and the disease (a predisposition is presupposed), we are not at all clear about this in dementia præcox. We do not know whether, in predisposed cases, it is the complex that causes or sets free the disease, or whether at the moment of the outbreak of the disease, a definite complex is present which determines the symptoms. The more detailed and sharper the analysis, the more we see that in numerous cases at the onset of the disease there was a strong affect from which the initiatory moodiness developed. In such cases one feels tempted to attribute causal significance to the complex, but one must add the already mentioned restriction, that is, that the complex, besides its psychological effects, produces also an X (toxin?) which helps along the process of destruction. Yet I am fully cognizant of the possibility that the X may primarily result from other than psychological reasons or causes, and then seize the last remaining complex and specifically change it, so that it may seem as if the complex had causal effects. Be this as it may, the psychological consequences remain the same, namely, the psyche never rids itself of the complex. With the desolation of the complex an improvement takes place, but this is also accompanied by a destruction of a more or less greater portion of the personality, so that the precocious dement at best escapes with a psychic mutilation. The separation of the precocious dement from reality, the loss of interest in objective happenings, is not difficult to explain when we consider that he persistently stands under the ban of an invincible complex. He whose whole interest is chained by a complex must be like one dead to all surroundings. Janet's normal "*fonction du réel*" must cease with it. He who is possessed by a strong complex continues to think in the complex, he dreams with open eyes and psychologically no more adapts himself to his surroundings. That which Janet says about the "*fonction du réel*" in hysteria is, in a certain measure, also true in dementia præcox: "The patient constructs in his imagination small, very coherent and very logical stories; it is when reality is to be dealt with that he is no more capable of paying attention or of understanding." The greatest difficulty in these really not simple problems is the hypothetic X, the metabolic toxin(?) and its effects on the psyche. It is uncommonly difficult to characterize, in a measure, these effects from the psychological side. If I may be allowed to give expression to a supposition I would say that to me it seems that the effects most distinctly manifest themselves in the enormous tendencies towards automatization and fixation; in other words, in the persistence of complex effects. Accordingly, the toxin(?) is to be considered as a highly developed body which adheres everywhere to the psychic processes, especially to those which are emotionally accentuated, reinforcing and automatizing them. Finally it must be considered that the complex to a great extent absorbs the brain activity, on account of which something like a deencephalization takes place. The results of this may be the origin of those forms of automatism which are principally developed in the motor system.

This more programmatic than exhaustive review of the parallels between hysteria and dementia præcox may probably sound hypothetical to those readers not accustomed to Freud's views. By no means do I intend to give here anything conclusive, but rather something preparatory in order to support and simplify the illustrations in the following experimental investigation.

CHAPTER V.

Anamnesis: B. St., seamstress, single, born in 1845. Patient was admitted to this hospital in 1887 and since then has remained continuously in the hospital. She is greatly tainted by heredity. Many years before admission she heard voices slandering her. For a time she intended to drown herself. She referred the voices to invisible telephones. She heard that she was a woman of doubtful character, that her child was found in the water closet, and that she stole scissors in order to pierce a child's eyes. (According to the anamnesis the patient led a thoroughly exemplary and quiet life.) The patient used here and there peculiar expressions. She generally employed a rather pretentious style. Her letters of that time will illustrate this:

July 5, 1887.

Dear Superintendent:

With these lines I request you once more to instantly discharge me. My head, as I already remarked to you in my last letter, is clearer than ever. What I have to suffer secretly on account of novelties in all domains is unfortunately known to me alone, and is too smashing for my health as well as for my mind. Unfortunately they have gone so far as to torture to death poor victims by secret cruelties, for I suffer more than you can imagine and in this manner fully expect my end, which sadly touches me more and more. I hope you will act in your place as physician and will have no need of any further reflection.

Yours respectfully, etc.

August 16, 1887.

Dear Sir:

Unfortunately I cannot make it possible for you to appreciate the sad conditions which have intruded themselves. I again call your attention to the simple fact, to discharge me without more ado, as I alone suffer under these novelties, and if you were to be convinced of it you would surely immediately discharge me, because I have suffered from the beginning since I came here, and am totally at the end of my health. I want an immediate discharge. It will be immediately better when I leave Zurich for another air where the horrors are not represented, etc.

The patient manifests active delusions. She has a fortune of millions, in the night her bed is full of needles. In 1888 her speech became more and more disconnected and her delusions less understood; she has for example the " monopoly." She makes peculiar gestures with her hands. A certain " Rubinstein " from St. Petersburg sends her money by the wagonload. In 1889 she complained that her spinal cord was torn out in the night time. " Back pains are caused by substances covered with magnetism which penetrate through the walls." The " monopoly " confirms the pains which " do not stick in the body and do not fly about in the air." " Extracts " are made by means of " inhalation of chemistry," etc. By means " of suffocation " legions are murdered. " Station for station must keep its proper governmental position so that existence-questions of the ward cannot be chosen to hide themselves behind, all things can be chosen."

In 1890–91 the delusions became more and more absurd, a great but incomprehensible rôle is played by the word " note-monopoly." In 1892 the patient became " queen of the orphans," " owner of the asylum Burghölzli," " Naples and I must provide the whole world with noodles." In 1894 patient at every visit asked for her discharge in a stereotyped and totally unemotional manner. In 1895 patient feels herself paralyzed and claims to have tuberculosis. She is the owner of a " seven-floored note factory with coal-raven-black windows, which signifies paralysis and starvation." In 1896 patient says, " I am Germania and Helvetia of exclusively sweet butter, but now I have no more any supply of butter not even as much as a fly would leave behind—hm—hm—hm—that is starvation—hm—hm." (The syllable " hm " is a characteristic stereotyped insertion which still exists.) She also says, " I am Noah's ark, the life boat and the esteem, Maria Stuart, Empress Alexander."

In 1897 patient relates that recently Dr. D. came out of her mouth "the little tiny D., the son of the Emperor Barbarossa."

In 1899 she was tormented nightly by many hundred thousands of snakes, etc.

From the extracts taken from patient's history one can easily recognize the nature of the case. At present the patient is as ever a diligent worker. She now and then gesticulates and whispers during her work. During the physicians' visits she puts her questions in a stereotyped and unemotional manner, such as "Have you heard nothing from the notes? I have so long ago established the monopoly, I am a triple world proprietress," etc. When she does not talk about her delusions her manner of expression and behavior show nothing abnormal, though there is a certain unmistakable prinking, not rarely seen in elderly unmarried women who strive to acquire an equivalent for unsatisfied sexuality by the greatest possible perfection. She naturally has no insight as to her disease, yet to a certain extent she finds it conceivable that her delusions are not understood. There is no imbecility. Her speech is changed only in the spheres of her delusions, otherwise she speaks in a normal manner. She repeats what she reads and defines ideas in a clear manner, insofar as they do not touch her complex. During the experiments and analyses the patient readily collaborated with the examiner, apparently taking the greatest pains to explain herself as well as possible. This behavior is especially due to the fact that the examination as such is also a complex-incitor, as the patient always demands interviews, hoping thereby to finally convince everybody, and thus reach the goal of her desires. The patient is always quiet and shows nothing striking in her general behavior. While at work she whispers to herself "power-words." These are stereotyped sentences or sentence-fragments of a quite strange content, such as: "Last evening I sat in the night train to Nice, I had to pass there through a triumphal arch—we have established all this as a threefold world proprietress—we are also the lilac-new-red-sea wonder," etc. Such fragments appear in great numbers, but are altogether stereotyped and can always be reproduced in the same form. Motor stereotypies but rarely occur. One stereotypy, for example, is a sudden extension of the arms, as though patient would wish to embrace some one.

Simple Word Associations.

For the last two years, at different times, I have taken from the patient simple word associations (corresponding to those discussed in the Diagnost. Assoz.-Stud.). I now present some of them:

Stimulus.	Reaction.	
1. Pupil	2. (This figure gives the number of repetitions of the antecedent word stimulus.) "Now you may write Socrates."........	12.4″
2. Father	Yes, mother	7.6″
3. Table ....1.	Sofa	3.8″
4. Head ....1.	Yes, irretrievable	14.8″
5. Ink ....1.	Nut water	9.0″
6. Needle ....1.	Thread	11.4″
7. Bread ....1.	Butter	3.4″
8. Lamp ....1.	Electricity, petroleum	6.4″
9. Tree ....1.	Fruit	6.0″
10. Mountain ....1.	Valleys	9.4″
11. Hair ....2.	Hat	6.2″

Among these repetitions some sound quite incomprehensible. Socrates, the first reaction to "pupil," is quite a striking reaction for a tailoress; it looks very affected and gives the appearance of a complex constellation. It also shows the tendency to affected speech and behavior. The same holds true for R. 8. "Lamp—electricity" (patient would like electricity instead of gas). R. 4 "yes irretrievable" to "head" is incomprehensible if one does not know that the word "irretrievable" is one of the patient's preferred stereotyped words. The reaction "nut water" to R. 5 "ink" is explained on subsequent questioning. Nut water is dark brown, ink is black. But how does patient get to nut water? It is again a complex constellation like Socrates. Nut water is something that patient likes very much. [It is made from the green shells of unripe nuts.] Besides these oddities one is struck by the numerous repetitions of the stimulus words, the unusually long reaction times, and the frequent beginning of the reaction with "yes." As is known we take these signs also as symptoms of complex constellations, it is the intervention of an emotionally strong idea feeling. But it must be realized that we deal with a patient with dementia præcox who presents her delusions (which according to our conceptions are nothing but complex-expressions) with marked want of emotion. If we really dealt here with a true want of emotion, it would at first sight seem contradictory that just here, where we always have the impression of an emotional defect, there should be signs of a vivid feeling tone. From numerous examinations in the normal and hysterical we know that these signs in experiments always, as it were, show the appearance of a complex, we therefore retain the same view in dementia præcox. The consequence of this supposition is that most of the above reactions are so to say constellated by complexes. That this is the case in R. 1 we have already seen. R. 2 " father—yes, mother " is designated by the complex-indicator " yes."[1] As we shall see later the parents play a certain rôle in the delusions of the patient. R. 3 " table—sofa " seems objective and has therefore a short reaction time. R. 4 " head—yes, irretrievable " has on the other hand again a very long reaction time. Patient refers " head " to herself and predicates this part of the body as " irretrievable," an expression which she otherwise applies to her own person and usually in the stereotyped formula, " I am double polytechnic irretrievable." R. 5 " ink—nut water " is a very far-fetched mediate complex-constellation. The patient, among other things, desires nut water. R. 6 " needle—thread " excites her trade-complex—she is a tailoress. R. 7 " bread—butter " is objective. R. 8 " lamp—electricity, petroleum " also belongs to her desiderata. R. 9 " tree—fruit " she likewise desires, she frequently complains about getting too little fruit. Occasionally she also dreams of a large gift of fruit. R. 10 " mountain—valleys." Mountain plays a great part in her delusions. She expresses it as follows in her stereotyped manner: " I created the highest pinnacle, Finsteraarhorn " [mountain near the Jungfrau], etc. R. 11 " hair—hat " should also contain a self-reference, but it has not been confirmed. We see then that by far most of the above associations are constellated by complexes, hence the objective signs of the feeling-tone are readily understood. What is not, however, understood at first sight is the unusually large number of complex-constellations. We see such an excess among the normal and hysterical only when the complex is extra-

---

[1] "Yes" as a complex indicator we found in an epileptic. See Beitrag III, Diagnost. Assoz.-Stud.

ordinarily accentuated, that is, when there is present a wholly fresh affect. But this is not the case with our patient, she is perfectly calm, she simply shows the results of the affects in the associations, the one-sided prominence of the complexes without the concomitant affective excitement. From this we receive the clinical impression of "lack of emotion." We still have the shells of the affect; the content, however, is gone. Perhaps the patient has misplaced the affect and these shells are only the wornout expressions for a repressed complex, having a more sensible and comprehensible content, but it is no longer reproducible and hence the affect, too, is buried. We wish here to call attention to these possibilities concerning which we shall speak later.

12. Wood ....1. Cushion .... 10.2"
13. Dream ....1. Reality .... 3.8"
14. Copy-book ....1. Map .... 14.4"
15. Paper ....1. Stamped paper² .... 5.0"
  ² Government paper.
16. Book ....1. Books .... 6.8"
17. Lead pencil ....1. Pens .... 7.6"
18. Sing ....1. Songstress .... 5.0"
19. Ring ....1. Band, union or engagement............. 16.4"
20. Tooth ....1. Set of teeth, teeth.................... 14.8"

R. 12 " wood—cushion " refers to her complaint that there are only wooden benches in the asylum; for her own use she desires padded furniture (" I establish upholstered furniture "). R. 13 " dream—reality ": Most of her delusions she takes from dreams, and when they are refuted she always emphasizes energetically the reality of all objects of her desire. R. 15 " paper— stamped paper " is connected with her delusions that there exists a state document about her enormous activities. R. 16 " book— books " refers to her stereotypy; " I saw the book awfully high above the grounds of the city hall," etc. This stereotypy likewise refers to her unusual activity, as we shall see below. The many reactions in R. 19 " ring band, union or engagement " show an especially strong feeling-tone. The erotic complex is here quite plain—it plays a great part, as we shall see later. R. 20 " tooth—set of teeth, teeth " also belongs to her wishes; she would like a new set of teeth.

21. Window ....I. Door, movable pane or ventilation....... 10.6″
22. Frog ....I. I like best paralysis.................... 18.2″
23. Flower ....I. Camelia .... 24.8″
24. Cherry ....I. Pear .... 9.8″
25. Asylum ....I. Causing .... 12.8″
26. Nurse ....I. Locked in .... 8.0″
27. Pianoforte ....I. Piano .... 4.8″
28. Oven ....I. Draughts of interest.................. 8.4″

S. 21 " window " has a multiform significance in her delusions, one of the most important is what she designates as " ventilation." She is nightly disturbed by fecal odors which she hopes to remove by better ventilation. The very odd reaction to S. 22 " frog " is explained by patient as follows: " A person is like that when he watches how a frog leaps, I always have such paralysis in my legs." " I have a paralysis," or " that is a paralysis " are stereotypies meant to indicate a feeling of paralysis in her legs. It can be seen how very far the patient leads the assimilations to her complexes. In S. 23 " flower " the reaction camelia again sounds as though affected. The camelia belongs to the ornaments of which she dreams. S. 24 " cherry " belongs to the fruit-complex. The remarkable R. 25 " asylum—causing " is explained by patient as follows. " Private people cause such asylums. I as world proprietress established this asylum but did not cause it, in spite of the fact that someone cried out that I did on my entrance." When patient was entering this asylum the voices told her that it was her fault that this asylum existed; she, however, denied this, but since then she has delusions of owning this asylum, for as " world proprietress all great buildings, so to say, are established as her property." R. 26 " nurse— locked in " is as shown by the reaction a perseverance of the preceding complex. R. 28 " oven—draughts of interest " is explained by patient as follows: " We are the ovens for the State, I am the lessor of interest-draughts." The last sentence is stereotyped—what it signifies we will see later. Reactions like " asylum—causing," " oven—draughts of interest," are certainly typical of dementia præcox, and are not found in any other psychic abnormality.

29. To promenade ...... 1. That means also for me an extraordinary
pleasure, when I can go out.
(Patient is allowed to go out once a
week.)
39. To cook .... 1. To roast .... 6.8″
40. Water .... 1. Lemonade .... 5.0″
41. To dance .... 1. Prim, I am Mr. Prim................. 10.0″

Here again a delusion is set free. Patient states that " Mr.
Prim is the first dancing teacher in Zurich." This name and
person are totally unknown to me; we probably deal here with a
delusional formation.

42. Cat .... 1. Slandering .... 21.8″

This far-fetched complex-constellation is explained by patient
as follows: " I was once slandered by somebody because I always carried cats in my arms." It is not ·clear whether the
slandering came from voices or from persons. The carrying
about of cats is not rare as a symptomatic action in erotic complexes (child!).

43. Heart .... 1. Reason .... 11.2″
44. To swim.......... 1. I was once almost drowned, to drown.

This is a recollection of a complex from the beginning of the
disease, when there were many ideas of suicide.

45. Emperor .... ˙Empress ....·............. 3.0″
46. Moon .... ˙Sun .... 2.8″

" I am Empress Alexander " is one of her stereotypies.

47. To strike .... 1. Is always a proof of rudeness.......... 15.8″

This refers to occasional attacks by other patients.

48. Star .... 1. Should one say, sun, moon, and all fixed
stars?

The complex constellated here is a delusion which is expressed
stereotypically as "I am Forel and Forel's star." [Forel—former
Superintendent of Burghölzli.]

49. To stroke .... 1. A word which can not be so well written:
to caress.

Here, too, an erotic complex is constellated; as probably also
in the above association. Both reactions came ·hesitatingly, with
introductions, showing a feeling of uncertainty, a " sentiment

d'incomplétude." This is probably due to a co-excitement of a strong unconscious complex, on account of which the conscious idea loses in clearness and completeness.

50. Splendid .... 1. Annoyance .... 6.6″

Again a far-fetched complex-constellation. Patient says one speaks though about unpleasant things, " that is really splendid." She finds it especially annoying that her fortune which she has long ago " established " is kept away from her " so imposingly."

51. Child .... 1. Parents .... 6.2″
52. Sweet .... 1. I have to experience the bitterness of life .... 11.0″
53. To ride .... 1. I must now be satisfied with driving.... 8.8″

Here patient again reacts egocentrically, that is, her complexes employ every available occasion to manifest themselves. R. 53 " to ride " also refers to a stereotypically expressed delusion. " I should have been horseback riding since 1866." This idea belongs to the grandiose delusions.

54. Friendly .... 1. Yes, friendly, lovely................... 12.8″

This refers to a stereotypically expressed grandiose delusion, " I am royally lovely, so lovely and so pure."

55. Crown .... 2. Villa .... 17.4″

Patient explains this as follows: " The villa S. in T. is my crown. I affirm it as my property." The villa S. is one of the finest villas in the suburbs of Zurich.

56. Rough .... 1. Is mostly rude .... 5.6″

An assimilation of the complex of rudeness (R. 47).

57. Ill .... 2. Ill is poverty

Patient explains that " poverty grows out of illness."

58. Victim .... 2. Cruelty .... 7.8″

As patient explains she is the " victim of unheard of cruelties."

59. Marriage .... 1. State affairs .... 7.8″

The marriage is an affair of state insofar as concerns her marriage, for she is the " world proprietress."

60. Grandmother .... 1. Is happiness .... 6.6″

Patient states that " where there is still a grandmother in a family there is happiness."

61. To quarrel .... 2. Always a sign of the dangerous........ 10.4"
62. Blue .... 1. Sky-blue .... 3.4"
63. Sofa .... 1. Pillow .... 7.2"
64. Thousand .... 1. 150,000 .... 7.0"

This sum corresponds to the amount of payment which patient daily expects.

65. To love .... 1. Great inconveniences .... 11.4"

She states that " people only love themselves," meaning thereby that no one cares about her demands and hence she must wait for her payments.

55. Wild .... 1. Indian .... 8.2"
56. Tears .... 1. Mourning .... 4.4"
57. War .... 1. I never caused any, always wretched.... 6.8"
58. Faithful .... 1. Imperishable .... 9.0"
59. Wonder .... 1. Summit .... 10.0"

Patient states: " It is not conceivable to others that I created the highest summit."

60. Blood .... 1. Ennobled .... 9.0"
61. Wreath .... 1. Is festal .... 7.0"

The first association is a distinct complex-constellation, the last is a fragment of her fancies which always occupy themselves with great festal occasions.

62. To part .... 1. Mostly causes .tears.................... 7.2"
63. Right .... 1. Righteousness .... 5.8"
64. Violence .... 1. Mostly it is cruelty, violent act......... 13.0"
65. Revenge .... 1. Quite natural in cruelty............... 14.2"
66. Little .... 1. Often it is a loss..................... 10.0"

Patient says: " If one has been great and then becomes little it is a loss." This refers to her grandiose ideas.

67. To pray .... 1. Is a " groundpostament " .... 11.4"

Patient explains this as follows: " Without religion no one can do anything great." " Groundpostament " is one of her preferred neologisms.

68. Unjust .... 1. Is always cruel....................... 8.2"
69. World .... World proprietress .... 4.2"

70. Strange ....1. Unknown .... 3.4″
71. Fruit ....1. Blessing .... 15.0″
72. False ....1. Bad .... 6.6″
73. Helmet ....3. Hero, heroic act...................... 11.4″

Patient compares herself and her acts to the greatest hero known in the world's history. She therefore uses helmet to express a complex expression.

74. To dress ....1. Taste .... 3.4″

Patient is a tailoress and always boasts of her excellent taste.

75. Gentle ....1. Tact ....,........... 6.0″

Patient says " if one passes through a bedroom one should walk gently, so as not to awaken the others."

Here we have a distinct constellation of the asylum life. She implicitly shows that she possesses the right tact.

76. Wretched ....1. Crutches .... 7.8″

This is a mediate association of " lame." Patient feels herself " paralyzed."

77. Hay ....1. Harvest .... 4.8″
78. Cleanly ....1. Good conditions .... 24.4″

Patient says " cleanliness creates good conditions," a general expression for implicit self praise.

79. Raspberry ....1. Sweetmeats, syrup..................... 3.8″

A part of her desiderata.

80. Head ....1. Wisdom .... 22.0″

This also belongs to the complex of her extraordinary intelligence.

I do not wish to heap up examples, for we can find all the essentials from those mentioned. We are struck before all, by the enormous number of quite clear complex-constellations. With few exceptions all associations are scantily veiled complex-expressions. Because the complexes stand everywhere prominently in the foreground we have the corresponding disturbances of the experiments. The extraordinary long reaction times throughout could be partially explained by the constantly encroaching complexes, a thing more rarely seen in the normal and even in the hysteric.   From this it can also be concluded that the patient's psychical activtiy is fully occupied by the complex.   She is under the yoke of the complex, she speaks, acts and dreams of nothing else but what the complex inspires.   There seems to exist some intellectual weakness which expresses itself in a tendency towards definitions, which, however, in contradistinction to the reactions of imbecility does not tend towards generalization,[8] but the content of the stimulus is defined or designated in the sense of the complex.   What is characteristic here is the unusual affectedness and embellishment of the expressions which often merge into incomprehensibility.   The awkward and peculiarly sounding definitions of imbeciles are found at situations which are intellectually somewhat difficult, where they are of course to be expected; but here the affected definitions appear in unexpected locations which accidentally stimulate the complex.   In the normal and hysteric we always see striking and disturbed reactions, such as unusual or foreign words, in the critical situations.   Corresponding to this we have here the neologisms which represent nothing else than especially forceful and rich expressions for the complex-thought.   Hence we also understand why the patient designates her neologisms as " power-words."   Wherever they appear they always refer to the whole system hidden behind them, similarly to technical terms in normal language.

We see then that the complex is connected with the most far-fetched words; it assimilates, as it were, everything.

In the normal and hysterical we see similar relations in complexes with very strong feeling-tones where the affect is still fresh.   In regard to the experiment the patient behaves like a person with a fresh affect.   In reality this is naturally not the case, but the effects on the associations are such as can only occur in strong affects; that is, by far most of the reactions are constellated in the clearest manner by subjective complexes. This fact is explained by the hypothesis constructed in the preceding chapters, namely, that in the content of dementia præcox there is an abnormally strong affect which becomes fixed at the onset of the disease. ·If this hypothesis be correct and holds true for all forms of dementia præcox we have to expect the associations in dementia præcox to be characterized by the presence of

[8] Comp. II Beitrag des Diagnost. Assoz.-Stud.

an abnormally strong complex. As far as my experience goes, this is really everywhere the case. In this point, too, we can see the great resemblance to hysteria. The complexes which have principally impressed themselves on this experiment are the following:

The complex of personal grandeur constellates most of the associations. It especially manifests itself in the embellishment which serves no other purpose than to raise the dignity of the personality. So far it is a normal and very familiar concomitant of self-sufficiency, but here it reaches an exaggerated height corresponding to the morbid degree of self-consciousness. Because the propelling affect lying at its foundation never apparently becomes extinguished, it remains for decades, becoming a mannerism and glaringly contrasting with reality. The same may also be seen among the normal who are unreasonably vain, and who retain their imposing attitudes even when the real situation in no way warrants it. Hand in hand with this exaggerated embellishment we find the exaggerated grandiose delusions which in view of their contrast with reality and also in consequence of their pretentious and indistinct expressions, show something of the grotesque. The principle of this manifestation we also find among normal persons whose self-consciousness contrasts with their intelligence and station. In the patient we again deal with an exaggeration which points to the conclusion that there is a corresponding deep affect. What goes beyond the normal mechanism is the difficulty of comprehension, and the inadequacy of expression which indicates injury to the fundamental conception. The complex of personal grandeur expresses itself also in inappropriate demands and wishes.[4]

The persecutory complex contrasts with the grandiose complex, and also manifests itself with great distinctness. In this disease it is the usual compensation for the greatness. Here, too, the expression is exaggerated and often difficult to understand and hence grotesque.

We also find some indications of an erotic complex which is, however, considerably concealed by the two former complexes. Yet it is possible that the erotic complex is the principal one; indeed in women one must expect it. Perhaps it is only charac-

[4] Patient continually makes absurd demands by asking for millions, etc.

teristically in the background, while the other complexes are nothing but its transferences.   We shall speak of this later.

A very sensitive person possessing an exaggerated self-consciousness will generally meet with many obstacles in life. This fact alone may be the reason for the complexes of grandeur and of being wronged.   But in this mechanism we do not find the specific cause.   We have to look for it among those symptoms which farthest deviate from the normal, that is, in the unintelligible.   Among the latter the neologisms stand first.   It is for this reason that I subjected the new speech formations of the patient to a special study, hoping thereby to find the clue to the essential.

Continuous Associations.

At first I attempted to have the patient explain to me what she meant by her neologisms.   This attempt was a total failure, for she immediately produced a series of fresh neologisms which resembled " word-salad."   She spoke in a self-confident tone, as if she were perfectly clear about the meaning of her words, and seemed to think that what she said was an explanation.   I then realized that direct questioning would lead to nought, just as in hysteria, when one interrogates directly as to the origin of symptoms.   I therefore made use of a means which is also applied in hysteria.   I asked patient to tell me all her thoughts evoked by the stimulus word.   In this manner it was possible to exhaust in every way the content of the idea and to learn its different relations.   As stimuli I employed the neologisms which are repeatedly used by the patient.   As the patient spoke very slowly in reference to her delusions, and was constantly disturbed by " thought deprivations " (complex-inhibitions) it could readily be literally transcribed.   I reproduce the tests verbatim, omitting, however, the repetitions.

A.   Wish-Fullfilment.

1. *Socrates*—scholar—books—wisdom—modesty—no words in order to express this wisdom—it is the highest groundpostament —his teachings—had to die on account of bad people—falsely accused—sublimest sublimity—self-satisfied—that is all Socrates —the fine learned world—no thread cut—I was the best tailoress, never had a piece of cloth on the floor—fine artist world—fine

professorship—is doubloon—twenty-five francs—that is the highest—prison—slandered by bad people—unreason—cruelty—excess—rudeness.

The thoughts did not follow smoothly, but were constantly inhibited by " thought-deprivation " which patient designated as an invisible force which always takes away just what she wishes to say. Thought-deprivation especially appears whenever she wishes to explain something conclusive. The conclusive is the complex. Thus we see in the above analysis that the essential appears only after having been preceded by a number of obscure analogies.[5] The object of the test is, as the patient knows, to explain the neologisms. If it takes her so long to reproduce the important phrase ("no thread cut") her imaginative faculty must suffer from a peculiar disturbance which can be best designated as deficiency in the faculty of discrimination between important and the unimportant material. The explanation of her stereotype " I am Socrates " or " I am Socratic " lies in the fact that she was the " best tailoress " " who never cut a thread " and " never had a piece of cloth on the floor." She is an " artist," a " professor " in her line. She is tortured, she is not recognized as world proprietress, etc., she is considered sick which is a " slander." She is " wise " and " modest." She has performed the " highest." All these are analogies to the life and end of Socrates. She therefore wishes to say " I am and suffer like Socrates." With a certain poetic license, characteristic in a moment of strong affect, she says directly " I am Socrates." The pathological part in this is the fact that the degree of her identification with Socrates is such that she cannot free herself from it. She takes her identification in a way as self-evident and presupposes so much reality for the metonymy that she expects everybody to understand it. Here we distinctly see the inability of discriminating between two ideas. Every normal person can differentiate between an assumed part or a metaphoric designation and his real personality, even if a vivid phantasy, i. e., an intense feeling-tone will for a time firmly adhere to such a dream or wish-formation. The correction finally comes with a reversal of feeling and with a readaptation to reality. The process is somewhat different in the unconscious. We saw, for example,

[5] Freud's analysis in the Psych. des Alltagslebens (Exoriar'alquis, etc.) is a prototype.

how the dream changed a metaphoric expression to a reality which it inserted into the personality of the dreamer, or, *e. g.,* an unconscious complex immediately condensed a distant analogy with the personality and thus attained the necessary intensity to disturb the conscious process, as in " A fir tree stood alone, etc." If in a brief dreamy state the unconscious complex could have reached the speech innervation he would have said " I am the fir tree." As was pointed out in the preceding chapters, the necessary presupposition for this condensation is the indistinctness of ideas as they normally exist in the unconsciousness. From the above source we explain the condensation in our case. As soon as the patient thinks in the complex she no more thinks with the normal energy, *i. e.,* distinctness, but her thought is indistinct and dreamy, as is normally the case in the unconscious or in the dream. As soon as the patient's associations reach the realms of the complex, the hierarchy of the chief ideas ceases and the stream of thought moves in dreamlike analogies, which, in the self-evidence of dreams, is put on an equal value with reality. The complex works here automatically following its laws of analogy. It is equally freed from the dominations of the ego-complex, and for that reason it is impossible for the ego-complex to properly direct the complex associations. On the contrary it is subjected to the complex and is constantly disturbed by defective reproductions (" thought-deprivation ") and by obsessive associations (pathological fancies). The same process of obscuration, which takes place in the ideas, is also found in the speech of the complex. It gradually becomes indistinct, similar expressions readily substitute one another and there are also sound displacements and mediate (speech) associations. Thus it makes no difference to the patient whether she says " artist " or " fine artist world," " professorship " instead of " professor," " fine learned world " instead of " learned tailoress." These conceptions substitute each other with the same facility as the patient's personality with Socrates. The accent is characteristically not on the simple but on the unusual, because that corresponds to the tendency towards external distinction.

2. *Double polytechnic* (stereotype: " I am double polytechnic irretrievable ") ; that is, the highest of the highest, the highest of tailoring, the highest accomplishment—the highest intelligence

—the highest accomplishment of the art of cooking—the highest accomplishment in all spheres—the double polytechnic is irretrievable—the universal with 20,000 francs—to cut no thread—fine artist world—not to apply lace trimming where nothing is seen—plum cake on an indian meal layer—it is of great importance—finest professorship—is a doubloon—twenty-five francs—snail museum clothing is the highest—parlor and bedroom—I should live there as double polytechnic.

The content of "double polytechnic" is very similar to "Socrates," only here the "arts" are more elevated. Next to the tailoring we have the cooking art with its specialities "plum cake on an indian meal layer." The art of tailoring reappears, as before, in the same stereotyped associations. It is quite evident that "polytechnic" is only another metonymy for the acme of art and wisdom. This is further determined by the "I should live there" meaning in the "polytechnic," as patient subsequently stated. At the same time it is no contradiction for either her consciousness or for the dream that she lives in the polytechnic as "double polytechnic." It is quite impossible to make her realize this incongruity, she simply answers with one of the above stereotypies. "The polytechnic is a government building" and hence "belongs to her." "Double" is an obscure epithet which perhaps resounds in "doubloon." Perhaps by this is meant the expected reward for this "highest" activity. "Double" may also have the sense of augmentation, or it may have another sense of which we shall speak later.

If the "double polytechnic" is the "highest," the epithet "irretrievable" then becomes clear.

3. *Professorship* (stereotype: "I am the finest professorship"). This is again the highest activity—double—twenty-five francs—I am double polytechnic irretrievable—professorship includes in itself the fine learned world—the finest world of art—I am also these titles—snail museum clothing, am I, that emanates from me—to cut no thread, to choose the best samples, those representing much—the finest learned world includes that in itself—to choose the best samples, those representing much, and consuming little cloth—I created that—that concerns me—the fine art world is, to apply the trimming where it can best be seen—plum cake on indian meal layer—the finest professorship is

double—twenty-five francs—it doesn't go any further, no one can earn more than twenty-five francs—snail museum clothing is the highest clothing—the others wish to bring together the learned world always with astronomy and everything possible.

The content of this idea " professorship " coincides with the two above analyzed ideas. " Professorship " is nothing but a further symbolic designation for the grandiose idea that the patient is the best tailoress. Through sound similarity " doubloon " is here replaced by " double," both expressions apparently have the same value for the patient. A doubloon corresponds to the value of twenty-five francs, and here it is clear that it means the highest day's wages that can be earned by labor. The expression " snail museum clothing " is a symbolic designation for the product of her art which she takes as the highest order of dress. It is explained as follows:· The museum is a place of rendezvous for the intellectual gatherings of Zurich; the house " To the Snail," a prominent guild hall, stands near the museum. These two presentations fuse together, forming the singular idea " snail museum clothing," which, as the patient says, designates also the highest type of clothing. Her manner of speech, too, is interesting; patient does not say " I make," but " I am the snail museum clothing, it emanates from me." She " condenses " or identifies herself also with this object, in so far as she treats with the same value the " I am " and " it emanates from me." The " I am " seems to be nothing but a reinforcement of the " I have " or " I make."

The three ideas thus far analyzed are technical terms which in brief designate (as it seems to the patient) in a pregnant manner an abundance of ideas and relations. Whenever she whispers to herself she simply repeats these terms and nods affirmatively, without adding any further explanations. The origin of these technical terms is unknown; some according to the patient come from dreams. Probably these expressions originated on some occasion spontaneously and on account of their strangeness were quite obvious to the patient, just as philosophers occupying themselves with obscure ideas readily play with obscure words.

4. *Summit:* sublimest sublimation—I am self satisfied—club-house " To the Plate "—the fine learned world—world of art—snail museum clothing—my right side—Nathan the Wise am I—

father, mother, brother, sisters, I have none in this world—an orphan child—am Socrates—Loreley—Schiller's Bell and the monopoly—God, Mary, mother of God—main key, the key in heaven—I always legalize our hymnbook with the gilt edge and the Bible—am proprietress of southerly zones—royally lovely, so lovely and so pure—in my single personality I am a von Stuart, von Muralt, von Planta, von Kugler—highest reasoning belongs to me—no one else should be dressed here—I legalize a second six floored note factory for the Socrates representation—the insane asylum should accept the Socrates representation, no more the former representation, which the parents had, but Socrates— this can be explained to you by a doctor—I am Germania and Helvetia from sweet butter—this is a life symbol—the highest summit I created—I saw the book awfully high over the city hall gardens, covered with white sugar—high in heaven, is the highest summit created—higher than the highest height—you can bring no one who can prove a mightier title.

In the conception of " summit " we find an enormous number of senseless ideas, some of which sound extraordinarily comical. From this material we see that the patient designates by " summit " the sum total of all her " titles " and activities. The subtitles such as Schiller's bell, Loreley, etc., probably designate special analogies which will have to be looked for in the special words.

5. *Loreley:* is world proprietress—it expresses the deepest mourning because the world is so depraved—a title which for the others is the greatest happiness—I might say that usually those personalities are extraordinarily tormented, who have the misfortune to be world proprietors—Loreley is also the highest living portrait—no higher memory can the world prove—no higher reverence—it is like a statue—for example the song runs " I know not what ere it presages "—it often happens that the title of world proprietor is not at all understood—that the people say, that they know not what it means, this is really a great misfortune—Yet I affirm the greatest silver island—that is a very old song, so old that the title didn't become known—that is mourning.

When the patient says " I am the Loreley " it is simply, as can be seen from the above analysis, a condensation of the connection of an awkward analogy, namely, the people do not know what world proprietress means; that is sad; the song reads " I know not," etc., hence patient is the Loreley.   It can be seen that it follows the type of the example of the " pine tree."

6. *Crown* (stereotype: " I am the crown "): greatest good-ness of life, which one can gain by conquest—those who accom-plish the highest come to the crown—highest fortune of life and goodness of earth—the greatest wealth of earth—it is all ac-quired—there are also lazy people who always remain poor—highest picture of heaven—the highest godliness—Mary, mother of God—the main key and a key in heaven with which one severs relations—I myself saw how a door was bolted—the key is neces-sary for irrefutable justice—title—Empress—world proprietress —highest merited nobility.

" Crown " is another analogy with " summit," but it expresses the nuances of the merits and rewards.   The reward is not, how-ever, consummated on this earth in the form of the gifts of the greatest earthly possessions such as wealth, crowning as empress, and merited nobility, but reaches into the religious heaven, into which patient is allowed to enter by means of a key and where she even becomes Empress of heaven.   In consideration of her merits this development seems to her " irrefutable justice."   A simple-minded dreamlike fragment which recalls to an extent the " Ascension of Hannele " (Hauptman).

7. *Main key* (stereotype: " I am the main key ")—the main key is the house key, I am not the house key but the house—the house belongs to me—yes, I am the main key, I affirm the main key as my property—it is a house key to fold—a key which can again unlock all doors—therefore it includes also the house in itself—it is a keystone—monopoly—Schiller's bell.

By this patient has reference to the pass key carried by the physicians.   With the stereotypy " I am the main key " she solves the complex of her confinement.   Here it can very well be seen how obscure her ideas as well as her expressions are; now she is the main key, now she only affirms it; likewise she is now the house, and now it belongs to her.   This key, which opens every-thing and frees her, gives her also the occasion for the analogy with the key to heaven, which opens for her the entrance to bliss.

8. *World proprietress* (stereotype: " I am threefold world proprietress "):   grand   hotel—hotel   establishment—omnibus—

theatrical performance—comedy—public parks—equipage—cab—
tramway—street mobile—houses—railway station—steamship—
railroad—post—telegraph—national holiday—musics—stores—
library—state—letters—monograms—postal cards—gondolas—
delegate—great occasions—payments—lordship—coach—negro on
the box—flags—one-horse carriage—open carriage—pavilion—
public instruction—banknote factory—mightiest silver island of
the world—gold—precious stones—pearls—rings—diamonds—
bank—central court—credit establishment—villa—male and female servants—carpets—curtains—mirrors, etc.

The picture which appears to patient at " world proprietress "
concerns the requisites of a princely existence, some of which are
situations carefully and most diligently pictured, such as " negro
on the box." These references give us an idea of the incessant
inner complex-activity of dementia præcox which objectively
makes itself known through a few unintelligible fragments. The
psychic activity reaches no more to the " *fonction du réel*," but
turns internally to an infinite thought elaboration which exhausts
itself in the building up of the complex.

9. *Interest draughts* (stereotype: " My interest draughts will
have to be accepted ") : cocoa, chocolate, noodles, macaroni, coffee, petroleum, black tea, green tea, sugar candy, white sugar,
nut water, red wine, honey cake, winecake—cloths, velvet, merino,
double merino, saxonian merino, alpaca, twilled goods, fustian,
white percale, shirt cloth, linen, wool, shoes, boots, socks, under-
shirts, underwear, coats, umbrellas, hats, jackets, mantles, gloves
—these are interest draughts which in reality belong to me.

The above is only a sample of the content of the " interest
draughts." We deal here with the concrete wishes of everyday
life, which have nothing to do with the " world proprietress "
complex. The imagination runs into the finest details and gives
the impression of careful assortment.

10. *To affirm:* to corroborate, to verify, to recommend—mostly
quite conclusion—to express an opinion—to take into consideration—what one affirms—to take in hand—the heathens chatter
so, the same thing is daily explained to them, yet they do nothing
in the matter—I affirm that I am paralyzed—nine years ago I
needed eighty thousand francs—payments through superintendent
Forel—they are rough to me—I affirmed the insane asylum sixfold as world proprietress.

The content of affirm is the same as mentioned above. The clearest meaning is in the sentence " I affirm that I am paralyzed." Here "affirm" has its exact and original sense. Mostly, however, patient uses " affirm " in a figurative sense as " I affirm the insane asylum " meaning " I affirm it as my property " or " I affirm a payment," meaning " I affirm that I have a claim on a payment." As was shown in the analysis of "main key" patient's speech is abnormally flexible and tends toward arbitrary and odd expressions. Normally changes in speech occur very slowly, here the changes take place rapidly and within the limits of the individual's life. The reason for these rapid changes seems to lie in the vagueness of her conceptions. She scarcely differentiates, and her conceptions are used and expressed now this way, now that way (compare " main key "). Judging by its content the sense of affirm is here very equivocal. Affirm contains corroborate, and verify, which at all events may be understood, although both terms go somewhat beyond the sense of affirm, but to recommend, to give one's opinion, and to take notice of, can no longer be logically connected with affirm unless it be as superficial associations. Both expressions do not in any way explain the sense of "affirmation," on the contrary they only cause it to become blurred. This is due to the fact that the presentations of the words are but indistinctly perceived and hence she does not recognize their dissimilarity.

11. *Universal* (stereotype: " I am the universal ") : I came as the universal seventeen years ago—universal firmly includes the reposal—regulated conditions—it is also by inheritance—it includes also wealth conditions—the title of world proprietress includes in itself one thousand millions—that is really the villa, equipage—since 1886 I was riding horseback and driving—I am universal since the death of my father—in the winter month I affirm the universal—even if I had not affirmed it in the dream I would have known it—on account of being a bequeathor—at least twenty-five thousand—with what an energy!—the Swiss life annuity is one hundred and fifty thousand—according to the telephone, Mr. O. drew my life annuity—universal is something definite—you can be that through deceased—through inheritance —universal is property—the property belongs to me.

According to these associations " universal " means universal heiress; at least this expression seems to be thus derived. The idea, however, is used quite promiscuously, now for persons and now for property. Again we have the same uncertainty. Instead of " affirm " patient prefers to use here " include " and on one occasion she condenses the two words into " festschliessen " (firmly include). The characteristic uncertainty exists also in her use of moods and tenses. Patient says, for example, " since 1886 I was riding horseback, etc."; she knows, however, quite well that this is not the case. On another occasion she says, " since 1886 I should have been riding horseback, but I adhered to driving." It makes no difference to her whether she expresses a subjunctive instead of a present or imperfect. She speaks as if in a dream. As is known, Freud[6] has pointed out this peculiarity in dreams. This clearly coincides with her other dreamlike, partially condensed and disconnected manner of speech.

" Universal " is another symbol of her wealth which she not only acquired herself, but also inherited. In this we also get a glimpse of her family whom, as we shall see later, she includes in her wish-dream.

12. *Hero:* I am a hero of the pen—pride—patience—heroic act—a hero of the pen, by the content of which, what one writes —the highest intelligence—the highest gifts of character—the highest perseverance—highest noblesse—the highest that the world shows—includes in itself—letters—business letters and letters of credit.

" Hero of the pen " is really a ludicrous expression which, however, the patient takes in earnest. Perhaps due to her deficient education, probably, however, because the comical has lost all its feeling, as is generally the case in dementia præcox. Furthermore this deficiency is also characteristic in the dream. " Hero " is another symbolic expression for " highest intelligence," etc. Her concluding remarks explain how much " hero of the pen " she is. The patient does not write anything except a letter on rare occasions. Her fancies, however, seem to be in favor of writing more letters, and especially " business letters and letters of credit," another requisite of her acquisition complex. Here it is also interesting to see how she expresses this distant thought symbolically by " hero."

[6] Die Traumdeutung, 1900.

13. *Conclusion:* alliance, counter-bill, closures, signatures, title-right, procuration—it mostly includes in itself the " key," the highest closures—dedication of the highest—adoration—I have dreamt that the adoration, reverence and admiration, of which I am worthy, cannot be brought to me—so wanders the noblest of women, with roses she would like to surround the people—Queen Louise of Prussia—I affirmed this long ago—I am that too—those are the highest conclusions in life—keystone.

The limits of the conception of " conclusions " is again very indistinct.   It seems to me that " counter bill, signature, procuration, title-right," etc., accentuate more the " validity " (Gültigkeit), while " closure, alliance and keystone " put forward more the " conclusiveness " or finality (Endgültige).   In reality these two relations merge into each other.   From " procuration " the association goes to " key " which, as we know, plays a great rôle as " main key," and regularly also evokes its symbolic counterpart, the " heavenly key."   Here, too, it goes from " key " to similar religious associations, such as " motto," which in her sense represents something " highest " and hence she can assimilate it.   From " motto " it goes via " dedication " to " adoration." In a former analysis the patient identified or " condensed " herself in a similar passage with " Mary, mother of God "; here it is only the " noblest " of women, the " Queen Louise," which is another symbol for her greatness.   She designates by this another acme of human virtue which, in addition to her other numerous attributes, she adds to the conception of " conclusion." This citation is a preferred complex-expression.

14. *Mountain peak* (stereotype: " I created the highest mountain peak ") : I effected the highest of all mountain peaks by mending—apparently this makes a sugar cone—it comes out quite white—one has to descend the mountain for meals—it was kingly—little houses are built on the slope—during clear weather one will go up there with tourists—it must be very remunerative —I, too, was there once—but the weather was bad—sea of fog— I wondered that such eminent inhabitants still remained up there —they had to descend for their meals—during pleasant weather it is very remunerative—it may also be thought that bad people are up there—the sense is royal because it is the best sense—if one has a royal sense it is excluded, that one should be killed and

robbed in such a place—yes, this is the mountain peak—the Finsteraarhorn.

The patient has long occupied herself with mending linen, she has mended enough linen to make a " whole mountain," " the highest mountain peak." Linen is white, hence " sugar cone."[7] The snowy mountains can be compared to sugar cones which are white on top and blue below, hence " Finsteraarhorn." Among these dreamlike but transparent associations the patient also inserts a dreamlike intermezzo about a mountain upon which prominent people live. Involuntarily one thinks of the Rigi peak, whose large hotels doubtless excited the covetous fancies of the patient. When subsequently asked about this intermezzo she states that she does not refer to any particular mountain, that she only dreamed of it. Nothing further could be elicited. She, however, talks about it as something real or as though it were a vision. Manifestly we again deal with an extraordinarily strong realization of a fanciful formation which occurs otherwise only in dreams.

15. *Turkey* (stereotype: " I am the finest Turkey "): I belong to the finest Turkey of the world—no other woman in the world can be drawn by lot—to choose—I am the owner of Champagne, and the strongest black wine—especially of the finest products—we are the mightiest preservers of the world—Switzerland as the most magnificent and mightiest state comes to my side—Biel, Liestal, Baden, Seefeld, Neumünster—no discord—Switzerland expresses itself in Turkey—the fine Turkey introduces the finest victuals—fine wine—cigars—much coffee, etc.

This recalls certain advertising pictures of Greek wine and Egyptian cigarettes, ornamented with the picture of a beautiful oriental girl (the patient also says, " I am an Egyptian "). Similar advertising pictures are also used for champagne. This is probably the source of these symbols. We again deal with some of her desiderata, such as " wine, coffee," etc. It also seems as if she imagines that she distributes all these things to humanity (" I am the bequeathor," etc.), perhaps only commercially, for such importation appears to her especially lucrative. She also " affirms businesses," as we shall see below. Be it as it may,

---

[7] Sugar comes from the refinery in the form of big heavy cones wrapped in white and blue paper.

what is essential for us is how figuratively the patient expresses
herself and how she assumes a geographical collective idea
(Turkey) as her title. This technical term expresses for her
the whole material mentioned.

16. *Silver* (stereotype: " I affirm the mightiest silver island in
the world "): speech is silver, silence is gold—silvery star—
moneys are suspended by silver—creation of moneys—the greatest silver island in the world—silver medals—one must adhere to
that out of which it is created—watches—silver snuff boxes—
curios—spoons—highest eloquence—speech is silver, silence is
gold—the mightiest silver island in the world belongs to me as
world proprietress—I afterwards gave the order to produce
money only, no external things—the already existing dishes will
have to be melted into money.

The silver island belongs to the requisites of the world proprietress, it is from there that her numerous millions come. Silver is, however, also speech; hence she also possesses the highest
eloquence. This example again shows quite clearly how indistinct her ideas are. One cannot really speak here of directed
associations, as these are only association principles of speech
combinations or of picture similarity.

17. *Zähringer*[8] (stereotype: " I am a Zähringer since 1886 ") :
Means paymaster—extraordinary health—often in life they say
you are tough!—I am a Zähringer since 1886—long life—extraordinary accomplishments—incredible with many people—it is in
the realm—one is so misunderstood—there are so many people
who always wish to be ill—they do not agree with the Zähringer
—quite extraordinary—highest age—do you know where the
Zähringer quarter is?—it is near the Franciscan church—a nice
quarter—extraordinary—ordinary people are not reminded by
this title—one often says they are so tough—this concerns the
state of health—it is such a great thing, this difference in age—
I am a Zähringer on account of health—that is extraordinary—
they often say what she accomplishes is to be admired—how
tough she is—in 1886 I affirmed this quarter, I have to live there.

The symbolic significance of Zähringer is clear. Patient is a
Zähringer because she is Zäh (tough). This sounds like a pun,
but to her this sound metonymy becomes reality. At the same

[8] Family name of Duke of Baden, Zah = tough.

time Zähringer also means to her a nice residence in the " Zähringer quarter." Again we have a dreamlike condensation of
the most multiform ideas.

18. Recently patient repeatedly uttered the following neologism: "I am a Switzerland." Analysis: Long since I affirmed
Switzerland as double—I do not belong here confined—I came
here free—he who is free from death and error retains a child's
pure soul—I am also a crane—one cannot confine Switzerland.

It is not difficult to see how patient is Switzerland: Switzerland is free—patient " came here free," hence she should not be
confined. The *tertium comparationis* " free " leads to a " contamination " with Switzerland. Similar but more grotesque is
the neologism " I am a crane." " He who is free from debt,"
etc., is the familiar quotation from the " Cranes of Ibykus."
Patient therefore identifies or " condenses " herself very rapidly
with " crane." The analysis thus far given concerns only symbols, of the unusualness, power, health, and virtue of patient.
They are purely thoughts of self-admiration and self-glorifica-
tion, which express themselves in enormous and hence grotesque
exaggerations. The fundamental thought: I am an excellent
tailoress, I have lived respectably and therefore claim respect and
financial reward, can be readily understood. We can also understand that these thoughts are the cause of many wishes, such as
recognition, praise, and financial provision for old age. Before
her disease patient was very poor and belonged to a family of
low station, her sister being a *puella publica*. Her thoughts and
desires express a striving to come out of this milieu and to attain
a better social standing; it is therefore no wonder that her wish
for money, etc., is especially accentuated. All strong wishes are
themes for dreams, in which they are represented as fulfilled,
not in the conception of reality, but in dreamlike obscure metaphors. In this patient the wish-fulfilling dreams go side by side
with the associations of the waking state. The inhibiting ability
of the ego-complex being destroyed by the disease, the complex
appears in the waking state and automatically spins its dreams
on the surface, in the same manner as it used to do under normal
conditions, only in the dim depths of the inhibited unconscious.
Dementia præcox has here pierced the investment of consciousness, that is, destroyed the function of the clearest purposive

associations, so that it is now possible to see from all sides the automatic workings of the unconscious complexes. What the patient and we see are only the complicated, distorted and displaced products of complex-ideations which are analogous to our dreams, wherein we only see the dream-picture but not the complex-thought hidden beneath it. Thus the patient takes her dream productions also as substantial and claims that they are realities. She acts just as we do in dreams, when we are no longer able to distinguish the connection between the logical and analogical. It is therefore the same to her whether she says " I am the double polytechnic " or " I am the best tailoress." When we speak about our dreams we speak as it were of something apart, we speak from the point of view of the waking state; when the patient talks about her dreams she speaks as if still in the dream. She is involved in the automatic machinery in which naturally all logically adjusted reproduction ceases. She is then thrown entirely upon her sudden fancies and is wholly dependent on the complex for any new reproductions. Accordingly, her stream of thought is burdened, constantly reiterating (perseverations), and is frequently interrupted by thought-deprivation which the patient considers very trying. If an explanation is asked the patient is able to reproduce only new dream fragments, so that no one is the wiser for it. She is unable to dominate the complex material and to reproduce it as if it were indifferent material.

From this analysis we see that the pathological dream has fulfilled the wishes and hopes of the patient in a most splendid manner. Where there is so much light there must also be shadow. Large estates of happiness must psychologically be bought dearly. We therefore come to another group of neologisms or delusions, which have to do with the contrasts, with the injuries or derogations.

B. THE IDEAS OF INJURY.

1. *Paralysis* (stereotype: " That is paralysis ") : bad victuals—overwork—sleep deprivation—telephone—these are the natural causes—consumption—backbone—from there comes the paralysis —rolling chairs, only these do they mention as paralysis—tortured—expresses itself in certain pains—that is the way it is with me—woe is not far away—I belong to the monopoly, to the pay-

ment—bank notes—in this the distress is affirmed—this is a right system—crutches—dust development—need immediate help.

Here we have the reverse of the medal. Just as on the one side the fancies lead automatically to every splendor, so on the other side we meet with all possible malicious persecution and suffering. It is for this reason that patient requests an indemnity which she expresses by "I belong to payment," which is synonymous with "the payment belongs to me." In consequence of her distress (Not) she claims bank notes (we shall refer to this pun later). Her complaints are of the physical injuries which are common to paranoid states. What the psychological root of the sufferings described may be I am unable to say.

2. *Hieroglyphical* (stereotype: "I suffer hieroglyphical"): Just now I suffer hieroglyphical. Mary (nurse) said that I should remain today in the other ward, Ida (nurse) said that she could not even do the patching, it was only due to my kindness that I did the patching—I am in my house and the others live with me—I affirm the asylum sixfold, not that I am capricious to remain here, I was forced to remain here—in the church yard I also affirmed the house—fourteen years I was confined so that my breath could nowhere come out—that is suffered hieroglyphically—this is the highest suffering—that not even the breath could come out—yet I affirm everything—and I don't even belong to a little chamber—that is suffering hieroglyphically—through speaking trumpets which are directed outward.

From this analysis, which was interrupted by an intermezzo with nurses, we are unable to see what she means by "hieroglyphical," though she illustrates by examples. During another analysis of this neologism she says "I suffer in an unknown manner that is hieroglyphical." This explanation is quite sensible. Hieroglyphics for the uneducated is the proverbial example for the incomprehensible. Patient does not understand why and to what end she suffers. It is a hieroglyphical suffering. To be confined for fourteen years so that "not even the breath could come out" seems nothing but a very exaggerated apostrophizing of her being forced to remain in the asylum. The suffering through "speaking trumpets which are directed outwards" seems to refer to the voices from the "telephone." Another interpretation may also be possible.

3. *Discord* (stereotype: " It is such a great discord ") : Discords—it is even criminal—I have to be cared for—I saw in a dream how two persons twisted two cords in the loft—these are two such big discords—I have to be cared for—discords can by no means go any more on this floor—it is too great discord that they don't wish to care for me—they made laces in the loft and worked on without thinking or caring for me—discords come from negligence—discords do not belong to this floor, but to Siberia—it is the highest time that I should be cared for, I have consumption—instead of providing for me now the bank title—they always continue to work—both have accidentally made laces in the loft.

" Discord " seems to express something like " precarious states." Patient especially feels precarious because the doctor never wishes to hear anything regarding the payment which she demands at each visit. She then mostly complains about the selfishness of humanity who only think of themselves and " always continue to work on " without thinking of the payment. The dreamlike intermezzo of the two men who were twisting two cords in the loft and " always continued to work " without thinking of caring for patient can be conceived as a symbol for the indifference with which patient is here treated. " Siberia " also points to the bad treatment. In spite of the splendid health which she on another occasion claims to enjoy she considers herself " consumptive." But just like all other self-evident absurdities these too do not conflict. Dementia præcox has also this in common with normal dreams. Moreover it can also be observed in hysterics and in somewhat emotional normal individuals ; as soon as they mention their complex they talk in a contradictory manner. The reproduction of complex-ideas is always disturbed in this or that direction or it is falsified. Judgment concerning the complexes is almost always somewhat clouded or uncertain. Everyone who occupies himself with psychoanalysis knows this.

4. *Monopoly* (stereotype: " I am Schiller's Bell and the monopoly or bank monopoly ") : With me it expresses itself in the bank note factory—very black windows—I saw that in my dream —that is paralysis—seven floored note factory—it is a double house, a front one, and the back is the residence—the note factory is real American—the factory is drawn into the monopoly

just as, for example, also Schiller's bell and the monopoly—the monopoly includes in itself all that can happen—all diseases which are due to chemical products, poisonings without seeing anyone, then attacks of suffocation—from above it is credible—again the awful extension—they always spread me out—with these victuals one cannot get such a figure—the awful system of burdening as if there were tons of iron plate on the back—then the poisoning, it is invisible—it is shot through the window—then as if one were in ice—the pains in the back, this too belongs to the mon-opoly—as Schiller's bell and monopoly Forel should have paid me eighty thousand nine years ago, because I had to pass through such pain—I am in need of immediate help—monopoly is a con-clusion of all innovations since 1886, chemistry productions, ven-tilations and sleep deprivations—a government would be forced without this to give immediate help—I affirm a note factory—even if I were not " world proprietress " the state would be com-pelled to bring help—as " world proprietress " I should have already fifteen years ago paid out with gentlemen through the note factory, forever, as long as I live—therefore it is such a great loss if one has to die only a year earlier—since 1886 the oleum belongs to me—all those who pass through such suffering, should be advanced, have to be advanced to the note factory, to the payment—such innovations are all comprehended in the word monopoly just as there are people who have the powder monopoly."

The sense of monopoly is again a very indistinct one. It is associated with a series of tortures. To this distress (Not) also belongs the " note factory." The patient emphasizes repeatedly that she needs immediate help. The often-mentioned " pay-ments " are connected with " she has to be advanced to payment on account of her great suffering. The probable trend of thought should be as follows: her unheard of and unique suffering, as well as her advanced age, demand that she should once for all be given her rights, which she probably designates by the idea " monopoly." The special content of monopoly is that patient as " world proprietress " is alone entitled to manufacture bank notes. The psychological connection is probably through the sound associations Not (distress)—notes.

5. *Note factory:* this is the creation of circumstances on

account of too great distress (Not)—the notes are of the same value as the moneys—all that is necessary to order—banknotes to alleviate the greatest (Not) distress—payments of wealth circumstances—I should with the town through life—the note factory should at all events be on our soil—I with four gentlemen should forever pay out with it—it would be a great loss to die one year earlier than is necessary, etc.

We can be satisfied with this fragment of the much longer analysis originally made. I believe it is clear whence the conception of " bank note factory " originates. Bank notes mitigate the (Not) distress. In this way another sound-symbolic connection was created, as so frequently happens in dreams. Thus one complex assimilates the other, and the two complexes are condensed in the words Not (distress) and bank notes, so that one conception always contains the other. It is quite characteristic of dreamlike ideation, that the most banal resemblances give cause for condensation. Two simultaneously existing complexes always blend also in normal conditions, especially in dreams, where the *tertium comparationis* may be any superficial resemblance. The money complex and the distress complex are both related as to contents; for this reason alone they must blend; distress (Not) and bank notes on account of their sound-association gain as to contents even greater significance. This type of thinking, as all psychiatrists know, is met with not only in dementia præcox, but in many other obscure manifestations. I call attention, for example, to the mystical interpretation of the name " Napoleon."

6. *Oleum:* belongs to the title " eternal "—it is for an old age —if I die, the title is gone, everything is gone—it is a somewhat longer duration of office of life—oleum serves toward prolonging —it belongs to me, but I don't know of what it is composed—one affirms the age—already since 1886.

Oleum seems to be an elixir of life which is to prolong the precious life of the patient. The expression " duration of office of life " is quite a characteristic pleonasm of patient. We see in this mainly the hazy thinking which joins together two totally different ideas. It also shows the pronounced tendency of patient to express herself as learnedly as possible (court language), a thing also common to many normal persons who strive to assume an air of special importance, as for instance in minor official reports. The pompous style of the courthouse or of half-educated journalists may under circumstances offer similar productions. Such individuals and the patient both exhibit a striving towards importance. The origin of the word " oleum " I do not know. The patient claims to have heard it from the voices just as she heard " monopoly." The creation of such productions is frequently due to fortuitous coincidences. (Compare " Japansünder.")

7. *Hufeland* (stereotype: " I affirm a million Hufeland left," etc.): Whoever belongs to Hufeland is universal, a millionaire— on a Monday between eleven and twelve o'clock I slept and affirmed a million Hufeland to the left on the last fragment of earth up on the hill—to this belong the highest qualities—wisdom —many people make themselves sick, this is really a great loss— as is known, one of the most prominent doctors, who affirms, what is true in life—seven eighths make themselves sick through unwise things—the million belongs in the realm of the million for distinction—a million on the last fragment of earth—you have also two sides doctor, that now concerns left—they would have had to pay me a million—this is extraordinary—the empty lazy people do not belong here—the money always goes into false hands—these are the deadly enemies of Hufeland, the empty, lazy, unwise—Hufeland is extraordinarily famous—to be a Hufeland is so mighty, to feel one's self quite healthy or quite sick, yes the will power does a lot—the highest essence of man is necessary in order to be Hufeland—perhaps doctor, you do not belong to Hufeland—Hufeland has no relations to cruelty, not at the present time—they also conditioned away my underskirt—and but only two bed sheets, that is unhufeland, that is murdered, if they make one violently ill—I once had an abstract from him, it is beautiful to read, how he agrees with every fiber of life—I am Hufeland—to Hufeland belong no cruelties.

Patient is " Hufeland "; we know her usage of speech and know, therefore, that that means that there is something in her relations which may be symbolically expressed by " Hufeland." She once read about Hufeland and therefore knows that he was a celebrated doctor. Perhaps she knows something of his " Makrobiotik," as is suggested by " will power does so much." It is unhufeland to take away her skirt and to receive only two bed sheets. In this manner she gets a cold, and this happens by the doctor's orders. Only a bad doctor who is no Hufeland can order such things. I was the physician and therefore she says: "You have also two sides doctor—perhaps you do not belong to Hufeland, doctor." The adjective "unhufeland" is most noteworthy, it has the meaning of "not in accordance with Hufeland." She employs the word "Hufeland" like a technical term, just as the surgeons say "We will do a Bier here" (sc. Bier's stasis) or a "Bassini" (sc. Bassini's operation), or, as the psychiatrists would say, "this is a Ganser" or "this symptom gives the impression of a Ganser" (sc. Ganser's symptom-complex). In the word "unhufeland," therefore, only the prefixed "un" is the pathological formation. The many complaints of the patient about unjust cruel treatment will justify the supposition that she wishes a "Hufeland" for her doctor. This thought may also be expressed quite well by the fact that she designates herself as "Hufeland": such a metonymy as we have seen is not at all unexpected. The idea of bad, unhygienic and dangerous treatment always associates with it "payment" which patient apparently conceives as a sort of indemnity. She does not make herself sick as seven eighths of the others do, but she is made "violently" sick. Probably for this reason a million should be paid to her. With this we approach the sense of her stereotype, "I affirm a million Hufeland to the left on the last fragment of earth," etc. The meaning of "left" in this stereotype is not quite clear to me. As in "oleum" we meet again the complex of death-expectation. The "Makrobiotik" is therefore a further nuance in the idea of Hufeland. The stereotype "I affirm a million Hufeland to the left on the last fragment of earth on the hill above" must therefore be a peculiar metaphoric paralogic condensation ("ellipse") for the sentence: For the bad treatment of the physicians which I have to endure here and with which I am tortured to death, I claim a high indemnity.

8. *Gessler* (stereotype: "I suffer under Gessler"): Gessler's head is set up here below, I saw it in the dream—Gessler is the greatest tyrant—I suffer under Gessler, William Tell is therefore the greatest tragedy in the world, on account of such personalities as Gessler—I shall tell you what he exacted of the people—he

demanded that they should have always the same linen and clothing and never the smallest coin—he was always for war, for battle—all cruelties, which these battles legalize—to cause, I suffer
under Gessler, he is a tyrant, there are people who are quite
inadmissible, of unnatural lack of reason and bloody cruelty.
For three fourths of a year I should have had trimmings on my
coat—it was only not given to me, that is Gessler, yes, Gessler—
bloody cruelty.

Patient uses the word " Gessler " just as she used " Hufeland "
as a technical term, with which she distinguishes the petty disturbances of everyday asylum life, under which she imagines she
suffers. The *tertium comparationis,* which this metaphor has
taken from " William Tell " is the humility which Gessler exacted from the people. It is interesting to see how this thought
immediately blends with the personal vexations of the patient.
Gessler does not demand of the people to greet the set up hat,
but " to have always the same linen and the same dresses."
Patient then assimilated completely the scene from William Tell
to her own complex.

9. *Schiller's bell* (stereotype: " I am Schiller's bell and the
monopoly ") : That is then—as Schiller's bell I am also the
monopoly—Schiller's bell is in need of immediate help—he who
achieved this is in need of immediate help—belong to the highest
title of the world—includes the greatest conclusion in itself—is
in need of immediate help. All who affirm this are at the end of
life and have worked themselves to death—immediate help is
necessary. Schiller is the most celebrated poet—for example
William Tell is the greatest tragedy—I suffer under Gessler—
that is really famous—the poem, the bell—this really affirms the
whole creation—creation of the world—this is the greatest conclusion. Schiller's bell is the creation—the highest conclusion—
that is a state's groundpostament—the world should now be in
the best of conditions—we have examined everything so practically and so thoroughly. Schiller's bell is the creation—the work
of powerful masters—the world was helped out of misery—it
should be in the best conditions.

. As can be readily seen the *tertium comparationis* is the greatness of the accomplishment. Schiller's masterpiece is the Bell;
the patient too has created something exceedingly great, hence

resembling Schiller's Bell. Following her familiar practice of
thought and speech the condensation takes place without any
further considerations, and the patient is then Schiller's Bell.
Because the patient now created her greatest and utmost work
("the world was helped out of misery"), therefore nothing
greater can follow, besides she is of advanced age. It is therefore no wonder that the complex of death-expectation becomes
manifested (even among normal persons at such an age it plays
no small part), and she then urges "immediate help," whereby
she naturally means the payment. By way of instructive intermezzo I may mention here that the patient took it very much
amiss of the former superintendent Forel because he did not
give her the "payments." Once during an analysis she said:
"I saw also in my dream how Mr. Forel was struck by a bullet
by means of which he caused his own death—that is really
awfully stupid—one has not always continued to do thus, if one
really affirmed the note factory." Patient rids herself of her
enemies by shooting them in her dreams. I mention this example, not because it is of interest for the psychology of our patient,
but because it is the usual typical way by which normal and morbid individuals rid themselves in their dreams of persons who
stand in their way. We can repeatedly confirm this in our
analysis of dreams.

I content myself with these nine analyses, they ought to suffice
for a general view of the patient's painfully accentuated complexes. Her principal sufferings play an important part, such
as "the burdening system" and the "paralysis," etc. The following thoughts express themselves in the stereotypies: she suffers under the discipline inflicted by the doctors and under the
treatment of the nurses. She is not recognized, and her merits
are not rewarded in spite of the fact that she created the best of
everything. Of great significance for the determination of various stereotypies is the complex of death-expectation which she
attempts to appease by "affirming" an elixir of life. A person
with vivid self-consciousness who was for any reason forced
into such a hopeless and morally annihilating situation would
probably dream in a similar manner. Every emotional and aspir-
ing individual experiences moments of doubt and apprehension
in the very hours of his keenest self-confidence, during which

any reverses of his hopes seem exceptionally heavy. The ideas of injury are therefore the usual compensation for over-estimation, and we rarely meet one without the other.

C. THE SEXUAL COMPLEX.

The analyses thus far have shown us in the main the obverse and reverse of the social aspirations, but we have not as yet encountered the most frequent and most usual complex manifestations, namely, those of sexuality. Wherever there exists such a richly developed complex symbolism there can be no lack of the sexual complex. Indeed it is present and is also perfectly developed, as will be seen in the following analyses.

1. *Stuart*—I have the honor to be a Stuart—it is so described, when I once mentioned it Dr. B. said, why she was beheaded— von Stuart, Empress Alexander, von Escher, von Muralt—this is also the greatest tragedy in the world—our all potent deity in heaven, the Roman Mr. St.[9] expressed himself in the most painful expressions, and with the greatest indignation about this most abominable intention of the world which pursues the life of the innocent beings—thus my eldest sister had to come here so innocently (from America) so as to die—then I saw her head on the side of the Roman deity in heaven—why it is abominable that a world should come to light which pursues the life of innocent beings—Miss S. caused me consumption—it is for that reason that I saw her lying in the hearse, a Mrs. Sch. whose fault it is that I am here was near her—it is incredible that the world is not freed from such monsters. Mary Stuart was also such an unfortunate who had to die innocently.

The last sentence shows clearly why patient happened to condense herself with Mary Stuart. We again have here an analogy only. Miss S. is an inmate of the asylum with whom patient could not agree. She therefore, like the other person who was the cause of her confinement, is in the " hearse." Whether we deal here with a delusion, a dream, or a hallucination makes no difference, it is the same mechanism as above (Forel). A remarkable figure in this analysis is the " Roman Mr. St., the most potent deity in heaven." We have seen above that patient bestows upon herself the title " God," we have therefore in this connection a firm association with the idea of deity. Here we

* Name of patient.

get another link, the name of the highest deity is " St." as is
also the name of patient. The predicate " Roman " probably has
to thank for its origin the vague analogy to " Pope." The deity
like the Pope is of masculine gender and differentiates itself from
the patient as " God." Next to the masculine deity, which name
is apparently meant to express a close relation to her family, she
sees the head of her deceased sister, a picture which reminds one
of the two pagan deities Jupiter and Juno. She therefore in a
way marries her sister to the godly Mr. St. This seems nothing
more than an analogy, it is a presagement of her own ascension,
where she will become (the sexually not indifferent) queen of
heaven, Mary, mother of God, symbolizing the earthly mother.
Such a sublimation of the very worldly matrimonial desire is,
since the oldest Christian epochs, a loving toy of woman's dreams.
From the Christian interpretation of the Song of Songs to the
secret rapture of St. Catherine of Siena and the marriage of
Hauptmann's " Hannele " it is always the same theme, it is the
prelude in heaven to the earthly comedy. To represent one's
own complexes in strange actors, as seen in dreams, is a recognized fact even by those investigators of dreams who absolutely
reject Freud's theories. As transitivismus it is not at all unknown in psychopathology. The above intrepretations I express
hypothetically, hoping to confirm them in the following analysis.

2. Stereotype: " I came at first with the deaf and dumb Mr.
W. from the city and first also with Uster." I came for example
at first with the deaf and dumb Mr. W. from the city—you go
here with Mrs. W. Uster—I am Uster—to guard against mistakes I state to you who must accept my interest draughts from
Uster—a Mr. Grimm—Uster, Jud, Ith, and Guggenbühl have to
accept my interest draughts—I came at first with the deaf and
dumb Mr. W. from the city and first also with Uster—that is
equal interest draughts—that is the equilibrium with the interest
draughts from Uster. I affirm the churches of the city to guard
the money. Mr. K. in M. manages my money in St. Peter.
There I see the deaf and dumb Mr. W. near St. Peter, in dream
one Sunday while I slept—Mr. W. can give information about
the last penny belonging to me. Mr. W. belongs to the city and
not to Uster—I came at first with the deaf and dumb Mr. W.
from the city and at first also with Uster—that is double—
equilibrium.

By "city" the patient naturally means Zürich. Uster is a small prosperous and industrious town near Zürich. Mr. W. is unknown to me, hence I cannot speak about his more intimate determinations. The essential content of the above analysis lies in the first three sentences. Mr. W. "can give information about the last penny" of patient. He is therefore in her dreams firmly associated with her wealth and indeed as it appears in the above analysis with her sums deposited in her Zürich churches. (The patient once dreamed that the church of St. Peter was filled for her up to the roof with five franc pieces.) This wealth is compared with that of Uster. We know already that everything pleasing to patient is affirmed. Among the things affirmed we find large business houses of the city, and among others the whole Bahnhof street of the town of Chur. It is therefore no wonder that she "affirms" also the prosperous factories in Uster, hence she says "I am Uster," she also says "I am Chur." Furthermore she said to me "You go with Mrs. W. Uster—I am Uster." This clears up matters. She simply indicates by this that she is married to Mr. W. Through this marriage she unites all the wealth of Zürich and Uster. "That is double equilibrium with the interest draught from Uster." I wish to recall the former use of "double" which was there incomprehensible; here we can attach to it a satisfying erotic sense. The marriage which in the former analysis was simply indicated by transcendental symbols is here effected in a rather prosaic manner. The real, I might say, the coarse symbols are still lacking. We shall, however, find them in the following analysis.

3. *Amphi.*—This word comes to the surface but rarely in the form of "doctor this is again too much amphi." Patient rather vaguely deduces this word from "amphibian." If she occasionally complains about being disturbed at night by amphi and when asked to explain it, she talks about "a ritze-ratze animal," which "gnaws the floor"; it is, however, impossible to discover what harm "amphi" occasions her.

Amphi—that expresses itself in hedge hog, so broad and so long (indicating about a foot in length and somewhat less in breadth)—one morning, Mr. Zuppinger, through pork sausages —now I don't know if the men purposely wish to bring to the world such an animal—I affirmed this through pork sausages—

I always hear: that is too much amphi. The animal might have become so big only through mistake—it must be in the evacuation (stool)—instead of a factory in S. there was a building for amphi—for productions—I saw in my dream in Weggen St. on an arch it was written "only by well replenished tables after supper"—I never saw such production—it requires a great building—one seemed like in a theater—there above—I think that all kinds of animals will be named—amphi expresses that the animals have probably human reason—they can make themselves understood like human beings—they are really amphibians, snakes and that kind—the hedge hog is so long (indicates with her hands a little less than a foot), and Sunday morning it came creeping to the well—yes, Mr. Zuppinger—that was through pork sausages—Mr. Zuppinger ate pork sausages. While I once affirmed in my dream 1,000 millions, a green little snake came as far as my mouth—it had the finest, loveliest sense, just as if it had human reason, and wished to tell me something—just as if it wished to kiss me (at the phrase " a green little snake " patient manifested vivid symptoms of affect, such as blushing and timid laughing).

From the peculiar content of this material we ought to understand without anything further what the meaning of amphi is. Amphi is manifestly an animal of oblong form, it creeps, it is associated with amphibians, snakes, hedge hogs, probably also with "pork sausages." Moreover amphi is also associated with " men " (" whether the men purposely wished to bring to the world such an animal "), and especially by pork sausages with " Mr. Zuppinger," about whom I was unable to obtain any more information from patient. The comparison of two passages will be of special value for the explanations.

The hedge hog is so long and came on Sunday morning, creeping up to the well—yes Mr. Zuppinger that was through " pork sausages." Mr. Zuppinger has ·eaten pork sausages.	While I once in my dream affirmed 1,000 millions, a green little snake came up to my mouth, it had the finest, loveliest sense, as if it had human reason and wished to say something, as if it wanted to kiss me.

It is no difficult task for the dream to condense, much less to make an analogy of two objects having an external resemblance. Such an analogy seems to exist between the kissing snake and the eating of pork sausages. The word " kiss " which produced a vivid affect in patient gives to the analogy the unmistakable sexual tinge. If a real plastic presentation is made of the process how the snake creeps to the mouth in order to kiss it, one will inevitably be struck by the symbol of coitus. According to the known mechanism of Freud " the transposition from below to above," this localization and interpretation of the act of coitus is a preferred one. This mechanism we have found in a number of both normal and psychological cases.[10] If the symbol of coitus is localized in the mouth the vague dreamlike fancy readily merges in the direction of eating, and it is for this reason that this act too is frequently drawn into the symbolism of coitus.[11] Hence it is readily understood why under this constellation the snake is changed into an edible sausage.[12] " Eating " should therefore be the analogue of kissing. The hedge hog plays the special part of an oblong animal. By its creeping to the well it seems to be blended with the snake presentation. Mouth, however, is represented by " well." Mouth can be understood as a sexual symbol if one assumes a " transposition from below to above," " well " on the contrary only if one assumes no transposition, but a figurative metaphoric designation on the basis of familiar analogy which the ancients have already applied to their fountains. Here then we encounter the " coarse sexual " symbols which we have thus far missed and which are as a rule extraordinarily prominent. Considering it from this point of view the individual details of the above association can be understood without any great difficulty. That " amphi " has human reason is not at all remarkable when it is meant to represent a man. Likewise can it be understood how the animal is " in the evacuation " (stool). There seems to be a vague analogy to an intestinal worm; the essential, however, is the localization of the symbol in the cloaca (Freud), which has already been expressed by another symbol, the " well." The obscure passage " only

---

[10] Compare, e. g., Beitrag VIII, Diagnost. Assoziations-Stud.

[11] See Beitrag VIII, Diagnost. Assoziations-Stud.

[12] " Sausage " is a familiar vulgar expression for penis.

after a well-replenished table after the supper " belongs to the
sexual symbolism of eating.   The nuptial night generally follows
a good supper.   As an old maid, the patient is able to say calmly,
" I never saw such a production."   In the expression " theater "
and " animals of all kinds," one gets the feeling as though there
is a presentation of a menagerie.   The expression " a factory
in S." also points to this, as S. near Zürich is the usual location
for menageries, carrousels, etc.

4. *Maria Theresa.*—I belong to the synagogue in Löwen street
since 1886, I am a Jewess since 1886—world proprietress—I am
therefore three Empresses—I am also Maria Theresa as von
Planta—that is conclusion—in my dream I was at a table with
omelets and dried plums—then there was a dam with speaking
trumpets in it—then there were four horses with mustaches over
their tails—they stood near the speaking trumpets—the third
Emperor has already legalized this—I am Emperor Francis from
the city of Vienna—in spite of that I am a woman—my Liesel
rises early and yodles in the morning—it is also there—every
horse stood near a speaking trumpet—(Patient suddenly goes
through the gestures of embracing someone and on being questioned she states that she once dreamed that a man took her in
his arms.)

This analysis, unlike the preceding one, was constantly interrupted by obstructions (thought-deprivations) and motor stereotypies (embracing), from which we may conclude that it concerns particularly markedly repressed thoughts.   The patient for
example described for some time with her index finger a circle
in the air, " she must show the speaking trumpets " or she designated small half moons with both hands " these are the mustaches."   Besides this the " telephone " made mocking remarks,
to which we shall return later.

By " Maria Theresa " patient again understands a particular
quality of her greatness.   This part of the analysis therefore
interests us no longer.   We have here a peculiar dream formation which ends with " I am Emperor Francis."   Emperor
Francis was the husband of Maria Theresa.   Patient is Maria
Theresa and at the same time Emperor Francis, " in spite of her
being a woman."   She condenses therefore the relations of both
persons into her own, which in her hazy way of talking probably

signifies nothing more than that both persons stand in connection to each other and that this has some resemblance to her. The erotic reference, especially the wish to have a distinguished husband, is very prominent. That it is most probably erotic we can see by the association immediately following which is an erotic song, " my Liesel rises early in the morning." This song is immediately followed by the horses which " stood near the speaking trumpets." Horses as well as bulls, dogs and cats appearing in dreams are often sexual symbols, because it is with these animals that one is likely to see the coarse sexual procedures, a thing which even impresses children. In a similar manner patient connects the horses with Emperor Francis. This justifies the suspicion of an erotic complex. The horses have " mustaches on their tails." This symbol probably represents the masculine genitals and thus we can explain their relation to " Emperor Francis," the symbolic husband. Every horse stands near a speaking trumpet in a " dam."[13] I took pains to discover whether the patient was acquainted with the anatomical meaning of the word dam, but I was unable to come to any conclusion without using suggestive questions. I am therefore leaving the question *in suspenso*. But considering the patient's otherwise fair education the fact that she might know the meaning cannot be disregarded. The sense of speaking trumpets would then be a very definite one. In the gesture of embracing and the mentioning of the sexual dream, the situation takes on a definite erotic coloring, which elucidates much of the dark symbolisms of the aforesaid pictures.

5. *Empress Alexander.*—That speaks of von Escher and von Muralt—world proprietress—as Empress Alexander I become the proprietress of the silver island—Mrs. F. told me that I must send one thousand milliards to the family of the Russian Czar —I have ordered that they should make money exclusively of the silver islands—I am three Empresses, von Stuart, von Muralt, von Planta and von Kugler—because I am world proprietress I am Empress Alexander—I am three excellencies—I am the highest Russian lady—catheter, chartreuse, schatedral, carreau—I saw a carreau (square) of white horses on the hill—under the skin they had the half moon like little locks—they were hungry—

---

[13] German word " Damm " can be translated as " dam " or " perineum."

Emperor von Muralt was also up there—I betrothed myself to him in my dream—these are Russians, that was a battle attack—on the horses were men like Mr. Sch. of U. with long lances—like a battle attack.

The first associations refer again to the grandiose ideas. The peculiar collection of sound associations like catheter, chartreuse, etc., leads over to a carreau of white horses, which although they had no half moon shaped mustaches over their tails, had however "half moons" under the skin "like little locks." We probably deal here with a similar but a more concealed sexual symbol. The horses are hungry; the association nearest to it is to eat. "Hunger" indicates a desire, perhaps a sexual desire (this recalls the sexual symbol "hungry dog" in Beitrag, VIII, Diagnost. Assoz.-Stud.). Unlike the former analysis the association does not touch the direct symbolic husband "Emperor Francis," but a similar distinguished synonym "Emperor von Muralt." The associations again go from the horse to the husband and this time the sexual reference to the man is obvious, inasmuch as patient asserts that she has betrothed herself to "Emperor von Muralt." The horses, too, now receive a characteristic attribute; they are mounted by men with "long lances"—like a battle attack. Whoever has analyzed dreams knows that whenever women dream of manly figures who come in the night into their rooms armed with daggers, swords, lances and revolvers, it is without exception a sexual symbol, in which the pricking or wounding weapons symbolically represent the penis. This dream symbolism can be encountered repeatedly in normal persons and in the diseased. I shall cite a case that I recently saw at the polyclinic. It is the case of a young girl who out of submission to her parents discontinued her love affair. She then suffered from depression with sporadic sexual excitements. Nightly she had stereotyped anxious dreams in which "someone" always came into the room with a long spear and struck her in the breast. In a similar case the patient repeatedly dreamed that she walked the street at night and that someone waylaid and shot her in the leg with a revolver. In dementia præcox we often find sensory hallucinations of knives in the genitals. The sexual significance of the horses in both this and the preceding analysis, as well as the meaning of "battle attack," ought to be quite obvious after

the above explanation. The transition of the associations to
" Russians " is not so remote in spite of the fact that mounted
lancers are at present quite an unknown spectacle in Switzerland. The " Russians," especially the Cossacks of Suwarow
from the days of the battle of Zürich, 1799, are, however, living
figures of popular tradition to which many reminiscences of the
older generations are attached. The " battle attack " is probably
a synonym for the embrace of the former analysis. The word
" hunger " probably conceals the thought of virile activity.

This analysis agrees in contents with the former, only the
speech and the figurative symbols are changed.

The analyses thus far occupy themselves with the betrothal,
wedding and coitus. The patient has plastically and forcefully
elaborated all the details of the wedding celebration; she summarizes it in the expression: " I am the lilac—new—red—sea
wonder and the blue." I withhold the representation of this
dream formation, not wishing to indefinitely increase this already
extensive analysis (the wedding celebration alone fills ten closely-
written folios). What we lack now is the result of this sexual
union, the children. These, however, appear in the following
analysis.

6. *Bazaar:* double bazaar—I affirm two bazaars—W. bazaar in
the Bahnhof St. and one on the strand—ladies work—the most
wonderful tinware, glassware, all jewels, toilet soaps, purses, etc.
Once in my dream Mr. Zuppinger shot out of my mouth as a
little doll boy—he had no uniform but the others had military
uniforms—these are Czars, the sons of the highest in Russia,
represented as Czars, therefore the word bazaar—bazaars are
extraordinarily good business—czars are dressed for such business, they have their incomes from these bazaars, because they
are the sons of world proprietors and proprietresses—also a
little girl jumped out of my mouth, with a little brown dress and
a little apron—the little daughter was allotted to me—oh, God,
the representation—it is the representation, the end of the insane
asylum came out of mouth—the little daughter was shot out of
the mouth until the end of the insane asylum—it is already
slightly paralyzed, sewn together with rags—it belongs to a
bazaar—do you know these businesses have a great income, I
came first as double, as the only world proprietress, first with

the deaf and dumb Mr. W. from the city and then with Uster— I am the double bazaar. (In a later partial repetition of the analysis patient says: " Both children look like dolls, their names I also have from the bazaar.")

As is shown by the contents of this analysis there is no doubt that the delusions also created children for the patient. The more intimate circumstances and determinations of these delusional formations are especially interesting. While prolixly enumerating the contents of the show cases of the bazaar (only slightly indicated above) patient stated that in her dreams Mr. Zuppinger shot out of her mouth as a little doll boy. It recalls the third analysis of this paragraph where Mr. Zuppinger is firmly associated with all kinds of sexual symbols. We apparently deal here with the results of these delusional references. This peculiar way of representation is historical with the patient. As early as in 1897 it is noted in patient's history that the first assistant, Dr. D., who was at that time revered by the patient, " came out of her mouth "; that is, " the very tiny D., the son of the Emperor Barbarossa." Dr. D. had a reddish beard which probably aided the formation of " Barbarossa." The advancement to the position of Emperor, which is probably a symbol of high estimation as well as veneration, has been transferred to Dr. von Muralt, the successor to Dr. D. (Emperor Muralt, with whom patient betrothed herself). The above passage can be easily conceived as the birth of a son from Dr. D. The event with Mr. Zuppinger is construed on the same plan. The manner of birth, that is, the child stepping out of her mouth, is an evident confirmation of the " transposition from below to above," and therefore firmly supports our view about the snake and the mouth as given under " amphi." That the little boy, Mr. Zuppinger, has some connection with this gentleman agrees perfectly with the sexual significance advanced above. Referring to the child as " little doll boy " is explained by its connection with " bazaar " in the show windows of which dolls can be frequently seen. Just as the mouth is a complex-representative for genitals, so is " doll " a more harmless complex-representative for " child," a thing quite usual in ordinary life. " He had no uniform on," " they are Czars," etc.—these sentences seem to contain a reminiscence from the preceding analysis, No. 5, where the critical

" battle attack " of the lancers stands in close associative connection with the " Russians," hence the transition to Czar. By sound-association the patient again finds the way back to " bazaar," a very characteristic train of thought in the obscure ideation of dementia præcox. The sentences " the bazaars are extraordinarily good business," and " the Czars have their incomes from these bazaars," in which is the sound-association Czar—bazaar, give to the patient an apparently sensible connection. She says " the sons of the highest in Russia represented as Czars, therefore the word bazaar." This formation is another " contamination." Patient " affirms " all bazaars as her property just as she " affirms " all good business houses. She is a Czarina just as she is all the other eminent personalities.

The special determination of this dignity emanates perhaps from the lancers. These two diverse trains of thought apparently flow together by clang-association, and so we have the Czars as owners of bazaars. As the " battle attack " of the lancers results in a son this son becomes a Czar and is furnished with a bazaar.

The strong tendency of dreams to analogical formations leads, just as in the other sexual symbols, to the formation of a second delusional birth, a little girl is born out of the mouth. It wears " a little brown dress with a little black apron." That is the way the patient generally dressed. This way of dressing has since long been displeasing to her; hence she often complains, and in her dreams she has already " affirmed " a very rich wardrobe. The passage " just as sewn together with rags " refers to this. The similarity of mother and daughter is crowned by the fact that the child is already slightly paralyzed. It is therefore subjected to the same afflictions as the patient. The child was allotted to her " as a representative," that is, by virtue of which resemblance it, so to speak, takes upon itself the vicissitudes of the patient. Through it the patient becomes absolved from the suffering of the insane asylum; hence patient can in a transposing sense say " the end of the insane asylum came out of my mouth." In another rather remotely transposed sense patient says that the child is the " Socrates representation." As will be recalled the patient identifies herself with Socrates, as he, just as she, was unjustly imprisoned and suffered. He was imprisoned, while she is in an insane asylum. The daughter then takes the part of Socrates, and hence she becomes a Socrates representation. This explains perfectly that peculiar and rather incomprehensible neologism. In order to complete the analogy the little daughter by way of indemnity receives a bazaar, as did also the son, the Czar. The idea of the double bestowing of bazaars leads to the expression of patient, " I came first as double—I am the double bazaar." She adds to it a well-known Uster stereotype which has a distinct sexual sense. " Double " may also have a variously determined sexual sense, that is, the sense of marriage.

In the further course of this analysis, which for the sake of brevity I have not reported *in extenso,* the patient continues to develop the thought of caring for her children and expands it also to include her parents who died in poverty. " With me the parents are dressed, the severely tried mother—I sat with her at the table—covered with white sheet—with abundance."

D. SUMMARY.

The preceding documents show us how the patient brought up under sad domestic conditions, amid distress and hard labor, creates in her insanity an enormously complicated, wholly confused and senseless fantastic formation. The analysis which we have made, precisely as we would a dream analysis, shows a material which is centered in certain " dreamy thoughts," that is, in thoughts which, considering the personality and circumstances, can psychologically be readily understood. The first division of the analysis discusses the afflictions and their symbols, the second the wishes and their realization in symbolic pictures and events, while the third division treats of the intimate erotic wishes and the solution of this problem in the resignation of her power and suffering to the children.

Like a poet impelled by his inner impulses, the patient pictures to us in her symptoms the hopes and disappointments of her life. The poet, however, even in his metaphors, speaks the language of the normal brain, and therefore most normal persons understand him and recognize in his psychic productions the true reflections of his joys and sorrows. Our patient, however, speaks as if in dreams—I know of no better expression. The nearest analogy to her method of thinking is that of normal dreams which make use of the same or at least similar psychological mechanisms, and which no one can understand without paying homage to Freud's analytic method. The poet creates by means of rich expressions and mostly consciously, his thought follows a definite trend, whereas this uneducated and scantily-endowed patient thinks without any directing idea, in obscure dreamlike pictures and amid indistinct expressions. All this contributes to making the stream of thought as incomprehensible as possible. That every person is unconsciously a poet—especially in dreams—is a banal expression. In dreams he coins his complexes into symbolic forms, to be sure, but it is only in an aphoristic manner, and it only seldom reaches a more extensive or a more connected formation, as this requires complexes of poetic—or hysteric force. In our patient, however, we have long and extensively elaborated fancies which on the one hand are comparable to a great poem and on the other to the romances and fantastic pictures of somnambulists. The waking state of our patient just like that of the poet, is filled with fanciful formations, while in somnambulists the extension and the elaboration of the system mostly results in the dissociated " other " state of consciousness. But just as somnambulists prefer to translate into exquisite fantastic and many mystic forms, and often allow their pictures to fade into dreamlike imperfections, so does our patient preferably express herself in monstrous and grotesquely distorted metaphors, which resemble much more the normal dream with its characteristic absurdities. What our patient has therefore in common with the " conscious " poet and the " unconscious " poet, the somnambulist, is only the extension and constant elaboration of the phantasms, while the absurd, the grotesque, in brief the lack of all that is beautiful, appears to be taken from the dream of the average normal person. The psyche of the patient stands therefore psychologically about midway between the psychic state of a normal dreamer and a somnambulist, but with the exception that through serious injury of the " *fonction du réel* " and adaptation to the surroundings, the dream persistently replaces the waking state. How dream formations may grow out of complexes I showed for the first time in the little book, " Zur Psychologie und Pathologie sogenannter okkulter Phänomene.[14]   I am obliged to refer the readers to this book, as it would lead me too far should I attempt to enter into this special domain.   Flournoy[15] has at least indicated the complex-roots of the dreams of the familiar Helene Smith.   For an understanding of the problems here touched upon I consider a knowledge of these phenomena indispensable.

The conscious psychic activity of the patient restricts itself to the creation of a systematic wish-fulfillment, as it were, as an equivalent for a life of labor and deprivation and for the depressing effects of an unhappy family milieu.

On the other hand the unconscious psychic activity is totally under the influence of the repressed contrasting complexes, on the one side under the complex of injury and derogation, on the other under the remaining fragments of normal censorship.[16] The entrance of fragments of these dissociated series into consciousness asserts itself principally in the shape of hallucinations in the manner described by Gross and from psychological roots as conjectured by Freud.

The associative phenomena correspond to the expositions of Pelletier, Stransky and Kraepelin.   The associations, though following a vague theme, are without any directing presentation, and therefore show all manifestations of the *"abaissement du niveau mental"* of Janet, viz., liberations of automatisms (thought-deprivation and pathological fancies) and the diminution of attention.   The result of the last is inability for clear presentations.   The presentations being indistinct, no proper differentiation takes place and hence there result many errors—condensations, contaminations, metaphors, etc.   The condensations result principally according to the laws of similarity of picture or sound, through which the connections of meaning are quite completely abolished.   The metaphoric variations of the complexes result in a near analogy on the one side to the normal dream, on the other to the wish-dreams of hysterical somnambulists.

The analysis of this case of paranoid dementia therefore confirms *in extenso* the theoretical hypotheses set forth in the antecedent chapter.

[14] Leipzig, 1902.
[15] Des Indes à la planète Mars.   Paris et Genève, 1900.
[16] Comp. Supplement.

E. Supplement.

In conclusion I take the privilege of calling attention to two special points. Let us first consider the expressions of speech. As is the case with normal speech, our patient's speech, too, shows a tendency to change. The new creations of language are in the main technical terms serving to designate in concise form certain complicated domains of ideation. In normal speech the formation of and habituation to new terms is usually a very slow process and their application is generally dependent on certain limits of intelligence and logic. The new speech formation and habituation process in the patient merged into a pathological acceleration and intensity reaching far beyond the understanding of her environment. The process of building up pathological terms shows a resemblance to the principles of change in normal language. Recall, for example, the changes of interpretation of the "Languedoc" dialect.[17] Many similar examples may be found in the history of language. Unfortunately I am not at home in this domain and do not dare search for further analogies. I feel, however, that a philologist would be able to make many important observations among patients with confused speech which would be of use in the study of the changes that have taken place in normal language in historical times.

Hallucinations of hearing play a particular part in the case of our patient. She elaborates her wishes of the day in the waking state, and at night in her dreams. It seems that she finds pleasure in this occupation, for it follows the direction corresponding to the inner inclinations of her personality. He whose thoughts run exclusively and perseveringly in a very definite and limited direction is forced to repress contrasting ideas.. We know that in normal persons, or at least in tolerably normal individuals, such as moody men, though the same mood may continue for a long time, it is apt to be interrupted suddenly by an invasion with almost elemental force from another sphere of thought. We see this in its highest development in hysterics with dissociation of consciousness, where one state is not seldom suddenly replaced by the contrasting one. The contrasting state often manifests itself through hallucinations or other automatisms

---

[17] Compare also Henry: Antinomies linguistiques. Bibliothèque de la Faculté des Lettres de Paris, 1896.

(comp. Flournoy), just as every split-off complex is wont to disturb the activity of another simultaneously existing complex. This may be compared to the disturbance caused by an invisible planet moving in the orbit of a visible one. The stronger the split-off complex, the more intensely will the automatic disturbances assert themselves. The best examples are offered by the so-called teleological hallucinations to illustrate which I should like to report three examples from my experience.

1. A patient in the first stages of progressive paralysis wished in his despair to kill himself by jumping from a high window. He got upon the window ledge, but at this moment there suddenly appeared in front of the window a powerful light, which practically threw him back into the room.

2. A psychopathic individual to whom, on account of some misfortunes, life became unbearable wished to commit suicide by inhaling gas from an open jet. He inhaled the gas forcibly for a few seconds, when he suddenly felt a heavy hand grasp him by the chest which threw him to the floor, where he gradually recovered from his fright. The hallucination was so impressive that the following day he could still indicate the place where he was grasped by the five fingers.

3. A Russian-Jew student, who later developed a paranoid form of dementia præcox, related to me the following: Under pressure of great unhappiness, he resolved to become converted to Christianity, although he was orthodox and entertained strong religious scruples against changing his faith. Finally, after a hard struggle, he determined to take the step. With this thought he fell asleep and dreamed that his dead mother appeared to him and admonished him against it. After his dream his religious scruples became stronger, so that he was unable to make up his mind to go over to Christianity. Thus he was wretchedly tormented for a few weeks longer until forced by his persistent distress he once more decided to apply for conversion. That night his mother again appeared to him in a dream and said, "If you do this I will choke you." This dream had such a terrifying effect on him that he definitely decided to desist from becoming a convert, and to escape his misery he emigrated to a foreign land. We see how in this case the repressed religious scruples made use of the strongest symbolic arguments, *i. e.,* the

veneration for the dead mother, and in this manner repressed the ego-complex.

The psychological life at all times is rich in such examples. As will be remembered, the Daemon of Socrates also played a teleological rôle. We may recall for example the anecdote in which the Daemon warned the philosopher against a herd of swine (in Flournoy we find similar examples). Dreams, the hallucinoses of normal life, are nothing more than a hallucinatory representation of repressed complexes. Thus we see that split-off thoughts have a tendency to crowd themselves into consciousness as hallucinations. It is therefore to be expected that we find in our patients that all contrasting complexes as a result of repression should effect consciousness by means of hallucinations. Their voices are therefore almost exclusively of a disagreeable and derogatory content, also the paræsthesias and other automatic phenomena have by preference a disagreeable character. As usual we also find in a patient near the complex of grandeur the one of injury or derogation. To the derogation also belongs the normal consorship of the grotesque grandiose ideas. That a censorship still exists seems *a priori* possible, for we see that patients who intellectually and emotionally are less well preserved than our patient still have an extensive insight into the disease. The censorship naturally contrasts with the grandiose complex which completely fills consciousness; it therefore probably acts from the repression by means of hallucinations. This really seems to be the case since at least some observations speak in favor of it. While the patient was telling me what a misfortune it would be for humanity if she as world proprietress should have to die before the payments the " telephone " suddenly said " it would do no harm, they would simply take another world proprietress."

While the patient during the association of the neologism " million Hufeland " was constantly troubled by thought-deprivation, and was unable to elicit anything definite, the " telephone " to the great chagrin of the patient called out " the doctor should not be bothered with such things." At the neologism " Zähringer," when the patient was having some difficulty with the associations, the " telephone " said " she is embarrassed and therefore she can say nothing." During an analysis when the

patient remarked that " she was Switzerland " and I was forced
to laugh, the. " telephone " called out " that is going somewhat
too far." During the association-test connected with the neologism " Maria Theresa," the patient was especially impeded and
I could not follow her; things were really too complicated. The
following colloquy took place:

Telephone: " You lead the doctor about the whole forest."

Patient: " Because it goes so far."

Telephone: " You are too smart."

At the neologism " Emperor Francis," the patient as usual
began to whisper, so that I could not understand her. She was
therefore required to repeat over aloud many sentences. I became somewhat nervous at this and told her impatiently to talk
louder, to which she answered rather irritably. The " tele-.
phone " then said " now they will probably begin to pull each
other's hair." Patient once said, emphatically, " I am the key
stone, the monopoly, and Schiller's Bell," to which the " telephone " remarked: " This is so important as to cause a drop in
the markets."

In these examples the " telephone " has the character of an
ironical correcting spectator or censor, who is thoroughly convinced of the uselessness of the morbid machinations, and therefore mocks the patient's assertions in a rather superior tone.
Such voices give the impression of a personified self-irony. Unfortunately in spite of zealous search I lack the necessary material for a closer characterization of this interesting dissociated
personality. But this small material allows us at least the con-
jecture that besides the complexes of grandeur and injury, there
exists still another complex which retains a certain normal censorship, but is prevented from reproduction by the complex of
grandeur, so that no direct intercourse can be had with it.
(Direct intercourse can be had with such personalities in somnambulists by means of automatic writing.)

This apparently three-fold division gives material for reflection, not only from the psychological, but also from the clinical
side of dementia præcox. In our case intercourse with the outer
world is controlled by the complex of grandeur. This could be
quasi-accidental. We know many cases where the reproductions
are controlled by the derogatory or persecutory complex and

where we receive only intimations of the presence of grandiose delusions. Finally there are cases where a certain corrective, ironical, and fairly normal ego-remnant is in evidence, while the other two complexes perform in the unconscious and are only made evident by hallucinations. Single cases may from time to time vary according to this scheme. In Schreber for example we see during convalescence the reassertion of itself by the critical ego-fragment.

CONCLUSION.

I do not imagine that I have offered anything conclusive in this work; this domain is too extensive and as yet too obscure for that. It would be far beyond the power of a single person to carry out in the course of a few years all the experimental work himself which alone could support my hypothetical views. I have to content myself with the hope that the above case of dementia præcox, analyzed as thoroughly as possible, will give the reader an idea of how we think and work here. If in addition to this he will consider the fundamental thoughts and experimental proofs of the " Diagnostischen Assoziationsstudien " he will perhaps be placed in a position to form for himself a detailed picture of the psychological point of view from which we study the morbid mental changes of dementia præcox. I am perfectly conscious of the fact that the above case only partially confirms the views presented in the preceding chapters and that it can only serve as a paradigm for certain kinds of paranoid dementia. It manifestly does not touch the wide domains of catatonia and hebephrenia. So far as relates to these I must prepare the reader to expect future contributions to the " Diagnostischen Assoziationsstudien " which will, I anticipate, contain some further experimental work in connection with the psychology of dementia præcox.

I have made it easy for the critics; my work has many weak points and gaps for which I beg the reader's kindly consideration. The critic, however, must be regardless in the interest of truth. Somebody had to take it upon himself at length to set the stone rolling.

www.ingramcontent.com/pod-product-compliance
Lightning Source LLC
Chambersburg PA
CBHW050842270326
41930CB00019B/3430